LEGAL BASICS

A Handbook for Educators

EVELYN B. KELLY

SECOND EDITION

Phi Delta Kappa International
Bloomington, Indiana U.S.A.

Cover design by
Victoria Voelker

Library of Congress Control Number 2006905120

Phi Delta Kappa International
408 North Union Street
Post Office Box 789
Bloomington, IN 47402-0789
U.S.A.

Printed in the United States of America
ISBN 0-87357-867-2

Table of Contents

Introduction

Test your knowledge of the law.

You are an elementary principal. Because there have been several incidents of weapons on campus, your school advisory council has demanded a tough "zero tolerance" policy regarding any type of weapon. A student who brings a weapon to school — with or without malicious intent — is to be given an immediate one-day suspension. A kindergarten teacher reports that one of her students has a metal fingernail file and is waving it around. The girl has a history of disruptive behavior. Is the fingernail file a weapon? What do you do?

* * *

A male teacher encourages his eighth-grade art students by patting them on the shoulder. One girl claims he patted her buttocks. The girl is a policeman's daughter; her father files charges. The school board initially places the teacher on leave with pay. Then, after a hearing, the teacher's status is reduced to leave without pay. Is this case about sexual harassment? Is it child abuse? What rights does the teacher have?

* * *

A teacher's aide is on playground duty when an elementary school student throws a rock that blinds another student. The rock is from the debris left from a school construction project two years earlier. The parents sue for negligence, claiming that the aide was not supervising the play area properly and that the rock should not have been there. What is the extent of the aide's responsibility? Is the rock really important to the case?

In the mountains of Colorado, road signs shout, "THINK!" This one-word admonition is designed to warn drivers that curving mountain roads are inherently dangerous and they need to think about their driving. Driving in the Colorado mountains is not the same as driving on a flat, straight road across neighboring

Kansas, where one might doze off for several miles to no great effect.

This is an exaggeration, of course. But my point is that hazardous conditions warrant close attention. Thus it might be well for every educator to post a personal "Think!" reminder. Superintendents, principals, counselors, teachers, and paraprofessionals need to pay close attention to their actions in schools and classrooms because, from a legal standpoint, those settings also may contain hazardous conditions. Almost every day the media show us the results of inattention to legal issues in the schools. Educators' careers are wrecked as easily as cars that slide off mountain roads into icy ravines.

The purpose of this handbook is to help educators at all levels recognize potential legal hazards in education settings and learn how to negotiate the slick roads safely.

Legal Basics is an apt title. The emphasis is on "basics." While degree programs for school administrators usually require at least a token class in school law, teacher preparation programs rarely do. And even the school law class for future principals and superintendents can be filled with legal jargon, Latin gobbledygook, and general cases that apply to state and federal laws, rather than practical information that can be useful from the administrator's first moments behind the big desk. Therefore I have chosen to focus more narrowly — and practically — on school and classroom issues.

Much of the information in this monograph came from interviews with school administrators, attorneys, law professors, and legislators and from my own teaching at Saint Leo University, where I teach educational law to both undergraduates and graduate students. The legal basics are discussed in the context of both informal anecdotes about actual situations and formal cases. All three of the scenes above, for example, are real cases that are discussed in later chapters. My hope in using this approach is that readers can envision themselves and their colleagues in such situations. If there is some chance that they might become embroiled in a similar predicament, then personalizing the cases in this manner may create a heightened awareness in readers of the need to understand the legal issues involved. This is an extension of the "Think!" strategy.

The first edition of *Legal Basics*, written in 1998, has been a popular Phi Delta Kappa book. This updated edition adds recent court cases and issues, as well as adding four chapters on issues not addressed in the first edition.

Chapter One describes how laws for education are made, and chapter two through eight focus on basic rights and responsibilities of educators, including speech, conduct, privacy issues, professional liability, classroom management, censorship, copyright, curriculum, supervision and discipline of students, property rights, and confidentiality reporting. Chapter Nine considers special education law, and Chapter Ten investigates the No Child Left Behind Act. Chapters Eleven and Twelve focus on chronic illness and sexual harassment issues. Chapter Thirteen tackles the all-important issue of religion in the schools. Chapter Fourteen relates to finance and negotiation. Chapter Fifteen has updated sources and websites.

This handbook is intentionally brief, but it covers a wealth of information that is important to the professional well-being of educators from kindergarten to high school, whether they work in a classroom, an office, or elsewhere in the school. Regardless of a book's length, however, no publication can substitute for competent legal counsel. *Legal Basics* offers information, not advice.

Chapter One

WHO MAKES LAWS FOR EDUCATORS?

Otto von Bismarck, the German Empire's first chancellor, said there are two things no one should ever see being made: sausage and laws. And a century ago, Bismarck had no idea how confusing, complex, and downright messy the process of making education laws could become.

The public schools of the United States are governed by a diverse set of laws. While public education is a state responsibility, the federal government and individual localities, through city councils and school boards, also take a hand in the oversight of schools. Therefore laws pertaining to schools and classrooms are established by a complex interplay among these levels of governance.

Perhaps the easiest way to understand who makes the laws for educators is to look at three sources of laws: constitutional law, statutory law, and common law.

Constitutional Law

Constitutional law refers not only to the federal Constitution but also to the individual state constitutions. The U.S. Constitution is the highest law of the nation and gives a broad framework for our way of life. However, the Constitution is silent on education.

The absence of a specific mention of education in the federal Constitution leaves open to interpretation the role of the federal government in the governance of education. But interpretations are the whispers in that silence. For example, Article I of the Constitution states, "The Congress shall have Power to. . . provide for. . . general Welfare of the United States." This "general welfare" clause has been interpreted to include the provision of public education. The Tenth Amendment to the Constitution defines, by default, the state's responsibility for education by stating, "The powers not delegated to the United States by the Constitution nor prohibited by it to the states, are reserved to the states respectively or to the people." Thus the states, from the beginning, have been responsible for public education, which means that the United States really has 50 "systems" of public schooling.

State responsibility for education is only somewhat more specifically stated in the various state constitutions. For example, Utah's constitution requires a "uniform school system." Virginia's requires that education be "free for all children."[1] However, some state constitutions establish the organization of the state's school system and define the rules of the state board of education, the role of the chief state school officer, how individual districts are to be organized, and so on.

Each state constitution represents the source of education laws for that state, and those laws are the "highest laws" of the state, provided that they do not conflict with the federal Constitution.

While there are many commonalities among the states, there also are many different organization patterns. In some states the state school board appoints the state superintendent, while in others the governor chooses the state's school leader. A few states still have an elected state superintendent.

Local school districts within states are organized in many different ways. A few states are single, statewide school districts. Some elect superintendents, others appoint superintendents. Some districts have school boards that are chosen in partisan elections; others have boards chosen by mayors or county or city councils. Local school districts range from very small, such as a village school system with only a few hundred students, to enormous, such as countywide systems or big-city districts.

Statutory Law

Statutory laws are those laws passed either by the federal Congress or by state legislatures. The involvement of the U.S. Congress in education legislation blossomed in the late 1950s. While such involvement is mostly "indirect," it is nonetheless powerful because it centers on standards and funding for specific education initiatives.

For example, when the Soviet Union launched Sputnik in 1957, Congress passed the National Defense Education Act (P.L. 85-864) with the aim to stimulate schools to improve math, science, and foreign language instruction. Later, civil rights proponents in the 1960s passed a number of laws that affected, and continue to affect, education. Examples include the Economic Opportunity Act (P.L. 88-4562) and the first Elementary and Secondary Education Act (ESEA, P.L. 89-109) that, among other provisions, funded Head Start, desegregation plans, and a range of compensatory education programs.

In the 1980s and 1990s Congress focused on what should be taught and who should teach it. Goals 2000 became the Educate America Act (P.L. 103-227) in 1994. And more recently, Congress has concentrated on national curriculum standards and national tests, further encroaching on prerogatives previously left wholly to state legislatures and local school district governing boards.

The "No Child Left Behind Act" was enacted as part of the reauthorization of the Elementary and Secondary Education Act of 1965. The final regulations became effective on 29 December 2002 and quickly became controversial because of items that seemed to conflict with state interests and IDEA provisions. On 3 December 2004 the president signed the Individuals with Disabilities Education Improvement Act of 2004 (IDEA 2004), which updated the sweeping changes of IDEA 1997 and clarified some of the provisions.

At the state level the laws promulgated by state legislatures flesh out a state's constitutional authority. Thus state statutes provide school funding formulas, establish basic conditions for schools (space requirements, length of school year), set teacher and administrator certification requirements, outline the duties of school boards, and so on.

The legal authority for the state to require attendance, immunization, or other programs that states deem essential is found in the common law doctrine of *parens patriae*. This precept says that the state has the prerogative to provide for the commonwealth of the state and for individual welfare. In a 1925 case, *Pierce v. Sisters of the Holy Names of Jesus and Mary*, the Supreme Court ruled that all children must attend school, but not necessarily public schools.[2] This decision declared an Oregon law unconstitutional that said parents must send children to public school, but it underscored the power of the state to regulate all schools and to require that children of certain ages must attend some school, whether public, private, religious, or home tutoring. The ruling said that a child has the right to be protected from abuses of parents and against the ignorance of his or her parents. The doctrine of *parens patriae* has been used in many cases supporting immunizations and various health education programs.

Common Law

Common law is not derived from specific statutes enacted by governing bodies, but rather developed over time through an accumulation of court decisions, customs, and general civic principles. Unless modified by statute (or by a constitutional amendment), common law generally prevails in cases related to education. For example, the concept of *in loco parentis* — that educators have the authority to act in place of the parent — still prevails in the majority of states. But various court decisions, not state statutes, have defined this legal principle.

There are two court systems: federal and state. Each system functions independently and applies its own laws according to the applicable statutes. Federal courts hear cases between citizens of different states and deal with litigation related to federal statutes or the Constitution. State courts hear cases on individual state or district matters. In some cases, of course, the jurisdiction (legal authority) of the two types of court overlaps; attorneys and judges must decide whether a federal or a state court is the appropriate authority.

First-Level Courts. The courts are arranged in hierarchies. The typical hierarchy in a state system begins with the lower-level court. The next level up is the appeals court and then the state supreme court. The federal court system begins with a lower-level federal court and moves to a federal appeals court. The federal Supreme Court is the top level for both federal and state court systems.

For example, if a civil dispute is taken to court, the district court (or first-level court) usually will be the first to hear the case. First-level courts have many names: trial court, county court, common pleas court, superior court, and so on. When reading cases, it is necessary to know the terminology of a state's legal system in order to determine the level of the hearing process. The person bringing the suit is called the "plaintiff," one who files a complaint. The "defendant" is the individual (or organization or group of individuals) being sued.

Court hearings involve numerous pretrial procedures, such as depositions or statements, interrogatories, and motions. Later, witnesses are called, testimony is given, and transcripts of the trial are presented as documents. In some cases the hearing is held before only a judge, in others it is held before a judge and jury. The first-level court usually is the only level that includes the full scope of a hearing with evidence and witnesses.

Appeals. If a first-level court ruling is not satisfactory, one of the parties may appeal. At this appellate, or second, level the attorneys argue their cases before an appellate judge (or panel of judges) using the transcripts and documents produced during the first-level court hearing. However, some states do not have an appeals court level, and so a case that merits appeal may be referred directly to that state's supreme court.

State supreme courts are the highest courts in the states. At this appeal level, attorneys present their cases from the written testimony from the lower-court trial(s). Supreme court justices hear cases and make rulings that must reflect a majority decision. The justices may agree with, or affirm, a lower-court decision, or they may reverse that decision.

Variations in terminology from state to state also affect what states call their high court. For example, Maryland's highest court is called the "court of appeals." In New York, the trial court is called "supreme court," and appeals are made to the "supreme court, appellate division," with the highest court called the "court of appeals." Pennsylvania has the most complex system. The first level is called the "court of common pleas." Depending on the circumstances, appeals go the "commonwealth court" or "superior court." The commonwealth court may be a trial or appellate court; the superior court is only appellate. The highest court is called the supreme court.[3]

Federal Supreme Court. The highest court of the land is the federal Supreme Court, which interprets the Constitution and, by that means, can exert a significant effect on public education. During the 1960s the Supreme Court was dubbed the "black-robed school board," hearing some 2,000 education cases between 1954 and 1970. The Court hears cases from state or federal appellate courts. Procedures are similar to the appellate court level in that attorneys argue the cases from written records of testimony. The Supreme Court accepts only those cases that at least four justices consider pertinent.

The U.S. Supreme Court has ruled that states may not enact laws or undertake activities that violate an individual's constitutional rights. Local school boards are agents of the state; thus school district employees are agents of the state when they are performing their school duties. Therefore local boards cannot enact rules that infringe on an individual's constitutional rights.

The Supreme Court is not mandated to review education cases. While Supreme Court rulings are the "last word" (short of federal legislative action in rare cases), important legal precedents also are established in trial and appeals courts. And courts at all levels may choose to send education cases to state boards of education, instead of dealing with them at the higher judicial level.

Most of the cases referred to in this book have been ruled at the appellate level or higher. A good reference for Supreme Court decisions is *A Digest of Supreme Court Decisions Affecting Education, Fourth Edition* (Phi Delta Kappa Educational Foundation, 2001). A regularly published source of legal information in education is "Courtside," a column in the *Phi Delta Kappan* written by Perry Zirkel, one of the authors of the *Digest.*

Freedom and the Law

The chapters that follow deal with issues that teachers, administrators, and others who work in or with schools need to understand. In each short chapter I have attempted to describe the pertinent issues and then to suggest legal points to consider. A central question is: Does teaching or administration require that educators shed certain rights on entering the schoolhouse door? The answer is, to some extent, both "yes" and "no."

Teachers and administrators do have certain "freedoms" that are protected by the Constitution or by statutory or common law. These include:

- Freedom of speech outside the school environment.
- Freedom of speech inside the classroom.
- Freedom from undue restrictions on personal appearance.
- Freedom to lead their lives in privacy.
- Freedom of association.
- Freedom of religion.
- Protection from arbitrary, capricious, or discriminatory actions or dismissal.
- Due process.

However, school authorities may impose "reasonable" restrictions that will limit some freedoms. When the courts decide matters related to the freedoms that I have listed, they balance individual rights against the needs of schools to effectively conduct the business of education.

Many cases turn on the way in which school authorities address the issues. Particularly when a reprimand or dismissal is considered, the procedures used to take action must follow commonly agreed-on standards, known as "due process." Therefore it may be most useful to conclude this introductory chapter with the last item on the preceding list.

Due Process

The Fourteenth Amendment guarantees: "No state shall. . . deprive any person of life, liberty, or property without due process of law." No concept of law is more basic to individual rights than due process. The purpose of due process is to extend justice and fairness to the individual in relation to government. This idea provides a fortress against the encroachment of the state on individual rights and interests and establishes a balance between the rights of individuals and the exercise of the power of the state.

There are two types of due process: procedural and substantive. Procedural due process involves the way that proceedings are conducted. Two parts are essential here: that no person should be condemned without a hearing and that every judge must be free from bias. A full and sufficient hearing must reveal the relevant facts required by due process. The person must be given notice and the opportunity to be heard before a final decision is made that would deprive him of life, liberty, or property.

Some people think that "due process" means that only employees who are about to be disciplined or dismissed must be given a hearing. The concept of substantive due process is more complex, requiring school boards to give employees a fair hearing whenever property and liberty interests are involved.

Property interests are involved whenever an educator is:

- Dismissed from a tenured position. Tenure, or continuing contract, is a privileged status given to teachers and some administrators by their state legislatures.[4] A tenured employee may not be removed without substantial "cause" (often referred to as "just cause") and then only through compliance with the established procedures. "Just cause" means that an employee cannot be dismissed for any reason that may be judged to be "arbitrary" or "capricious." However, tenure rights vary dramatically from state to state.
- Dismissed during the term of a contract. Except in cases where the employee fails to perform his or her job or otherwise acts in a manner that would subject him or her to dismissal proceedings, an employee cannot be dismissed during the term of a contract. For example, a principal can not decide at mid-year that he or she has found someone who will do a better job and then replace an employee under contract. Absent a "cause," this behavior would be regarded as arbitrary and capricious.
- Dismissed when there is a clearly implied promise of continued employment. A teacher has been assured of a teaching position in the coming year, but the principal decides during the summer that a coach is needed and the teacher does not qualify. The teacher still must be given the job that was promised. The principal cannot decide to hire a different teacher — in other words, one who also can coach — as that decision would be regarded as arbitrary.

Another notion that is involved in due process is "liberty." In some cases an employee may have a liberty interest in the action to reprimand or dismiss. *Board of Regents* v. *Roth* (1972) broadly construed the meaning of liberty and stated that a reprimanded or dismissed employee has a liberty interest in:

1. A public charge that might seriously damage a teacher's standing and association in the community, or
2. A charge that would impose a stigma or other disability,

such as to foreclose a range of opportunities for that teacher.[5]

In cases involving tenured teachers, most due process hearings are formal in nature. But for cases involving nonrenewal of non-tenured educators, due process may involve little more than an informal hearing. When there is no liberty interest involved, a nontenured teacher whose contract is not being renewed is not entitled to a formal hearing or even a statement of reasons, unless these actions are required by local policies or labor contracts. This last point is made clear in *Scott* v. *Oklahoma Board of Education* (1980), in which nontenured teachers were given notice of nonrenewal only a short time before they had completed three years of teaching. The teachers, believing that they had been treated unfairly, went to court. However, the court decided that the teachers were not entitled to due process hearings as no liberty interest was involved in the decision to let them go.[6]

Notes

1. Arthea J. Reed and Verna E. Bergemann, *In the Classroom: An Introduction to Education* (Asheville, S.C.: Dushkin, 1995), pp. 18-19.
2. Pierce v. Society of the Sisters of the Holy Names of Jesus and Mary, 268 U.S. 510 (1925).
3. A useful source of information on the court system is the *1997 Deskbook Encyclopedia of American School Law* (Rosemount, Minn.: Data Research, 1997).
4. Bernland v. Special School Dist. No. 1, 304 N.W.2d 809 (Minn. 1981).
5. Board of Regents v. Roth, 408 U.S. 564 (1972).
6. Scott v. Oklahoma Board of Education, 618 P.2d 410 (Okla. App. 1980).

Chapter Two

FREEDOM OF EXPRESSION IN SPEECH, CONDUCT, AND ASSOCIATION

An Illinois teacher was dismissed for writing a letter to the school board that questioned the methods used by the school board and superintendent to raise money for academic and athletic programs. The letter also stated that the superintendent was trying to keep teachers from criticizing a proposed bond issue. When she was dismissed, she took the board to court. What happened?

Freedom and teacher rights are topics that are not generally understood. The law relating to the rights of teachers is far from the minds of busy teachers and administrators working daily at their jobs. Some teachers are frightened to make any comments because they fear they will be fired; others perceive that freedom means that they can act or behave in any way that they desire. But courts have ruled that educators, as well as students, do not shed their constitutional rights when they enter the schoolhouse gates.

What actually can a teacher or administrator do or say? Once educators were the victims of arbitrary rules and regulations, but today's teachers' constitutional rights have been tried in the fires of the courts. Unfortunately, most are not aware of their rights.

Consider these questions: Are employees free to criticize their employers? Can a teacher criticize the principal? the superintendent? the school board?

Are employees free to dress in whatever manner they choose? Must employees conduct themselves in prescribed ways during their private lives? Are they constrained from certain behaviors, even in private, because they are educators?

Finally, are educators free to associate with whomever they choose? Can they join, or choose not to join, groups or organizations based solely on their personal interests?

Freedom of Speech

Does a teacher have the right to speak against the superintendent and the school board? Both administrators and teachers need to be aware of the case described at the beginning of this chapter, which was decided by the Supreme Court in 1968.

The Supreme Court ruled that teachers could not be dismissed for public criticism of their school system. In fact, the decision said that teachers, as knowledgeable members of a community, are most likely to be informed and have valid professional opinions. Thus they should be free to speak of such matters without fear of retaliation.[1]

The Court provided guidelines for evaluating public employees' free speech:

- Employees are entitled to constitutional protection on matters of public concern.
- Public officials are barred from recovering damages from defamatory statements unless the statements are made with reckless regard to the truth and the teacher's comments are detrimental to the system, rather than constituting only a difference of opinion.

However, the Court's decision did state a limitation on the right to publicly criticize immediate superiors that the teacher "would normally be in contact with in the course of daily work." Although the Court determined that the relationship between a teacher and the board of education or the superintendent was not a close working relationship, the justices believed that criticism of an immediate supervisor (a principal, in the case of a class-room teacher) could seriously undermine the effectiveness of the working relationship. Thus such criticism could legitimately be limited without damaging the basic right of free speech.

The first guideline above is a key principle in the area of free speech: School employees may speak out on matters that concern the public interest and are not simply school matters. A more recent case that ended up in court in 1994 illustrates this point. A teacher criticized a Mississippi school district for canceling the art program at a historically black junior high school. In several public meetings the teacher also criticized the superintendent's vindictive and retaliatory style of management. The superintendent then re-assigned the teacher to the junior high school saying, "Well, I thought you'd want to go . . . as much fuss as you kicked up over this."

The teacher sued the board, several administrators, and the superintendent, charging that the transfer was in direct retaliation for his public criticism and violated his rights under the Free Speech Clause of the Constitution. The Fifth Circuit Court of Appeals agreed and ruled that the teacher's criticism was pro-tected because it dealt with a matter of public concern. The court then found the teacher's case strong enough to present to a jury for consideration of monetary damages.[2]

These cases raise a couple of points that school administrators would do well to keep in mind. The first is to accept criticism from students and staff. They are close to the school situation and are entitled to voice their opinions about matters that concern them. If the criticism is unfounded or incorrect, then officials must present the facts and clear the air. If the criticism is valid, then school leaders must take steps to solve the problem.

The second point is that school administrators must be aware of any actions that might be construed as retaliatory or vindictive. When an employee has criticized a supervisor or other school official, any subsequent action involving that employee — repri-mand, transfer, dismissal — will likely be examined critically in any later court proceedings. Therefore school officials should

carefully consider their motives for disciplinary or other employ-
ment-related actions and be certain that such actions will stand up
to judicial scrutiny.

Many free speech problems can be solved before they become
matters for litigation simply by attending to good communication. Everyone involved in and with schools — from students to
staff, principals to parents — needs to practice good communication.
An aspect of that good communication is bringing grievances to
light at the level where they can best be solved.

In *The Rights of Teachers*, David Rubin, writing for the American Civil Liberties Union (ACLU), argues that educators are
protected in bringing problems in a school system to the attention
of their superiors but warns that educators must try all grievance
procedures before "going public."[3]

The courts have affirmed that teachers do have a right to address grievances. A class of second-graders wrote a letter to the
lunchroom supervisor asking that raw, rather than cooked, carrots
be served because of their nutritional value. Also, when a drinking fountain went unrepaired, the students presented pictures of
wilted flowers and children begging for water to the principal.
The students' teacher was dismissed as a result of her students'
actions. Subsequently, the court found "the school board policy
arbitrary and unreasonable; the First and Fourteenth Amendments guarantee rights of free speech to petition for redress of
grievances."[4]

Another incident provides an example that also is pertinent to
dealing with grievances. Agreeing with students' complaints
about the lunchroom, an eighth-grade English teacher assigned
the students to write letters to the local newspaper editor. The students wrote picturesque descriptions, such as "the wieners are
like rubber dolls' legs" and "the tater tots bounce off the floor."
The best letters were mailed to the newspaper. The principal first
became aware of the letter campaign when he read the newspaper. The lunchroom supervisor was embarrassed. Although the
teacher was not dismissed and no court action was taken, the
problem might have been solved without incident had the teacher

and the students dealt with their grievances through in-school grievance procedures *before* making them public.

That principle should be applied in even broader terms. In all matters of criticism, basic communication can solve problems before they reach a crisis point.

Freedom in Conduct

One's manner of dress and grooming, use of makeup, and other aspects of personal appearance are expressions of freedom of conduct.

While a school may not be the place for fashion trendsetters, acceptable dress and other personal appearance characteristics have changed with the times. They also vary from place to place. What may be acceptable in California can be seen as unacceptable in Kansas, for example. Regardless of locale, however, many schools upheld fairly rigid dress codes until the 1970s, when such codes were assailed from all directions — by teachers, administrators, parents, and students alike. Since that time, the standards for students' and educators' appearance have depended on the standard of "reasonableness." For the most part, the courts will uphold dress codes only if they address disruptive, unsafe, unhealthy, or immoral attire or appearance. Regulation of dress must be tied to the effect of one's personal appearance on learning (for students) or job performance (for educators).

During the 1970s a French teacher in Massachusetts claimed she was terminated because she wore short skirts. The school board denied this claim and said the dismissal was because of the teacher's lack of professional growth *and* poor image. The U.S. Court of Appeals acknowledged that personal appearance is guaranteed under the Fourteenth Amendment. However, it upheld the dismissal, quoting a similar case: "If a school board should correctly conclude dress has an adverse impact on the educational process, and if that conclusion conflicts with the teacher's interest in selecting a lifestyle, we have no doubt that the interest of the teacher is subordinate to the public interest."[5]

Of course, one can alter one's dress to conform to the requirements of the school, but what about hair length. In general, the courts have not supported rules regulating hair length, because doing so would give boards of education (or superintendents or principals) control of a person's appearance both in and out of school. Schools can require students to keep their hair under control for safety reasons (in a hat or a net, as in a cooking class, for example), but they cannot require that the students cut their hair. But decisions about hair have been far from universal. For example, in the 1970s a Tennessee school board dismissed a teacher for wearing a full beard. The supreme court of Tennessee determined that it was within the school board's discretion to decide if the beard would be disruptive to the educational process. While the teacher had a right to wear a beard, he could be denied the right in the context of the classroom.[6]

On the other hand, when personal appearance is an expression of heritage, race, or culture and does not impair the educational process, the courts grant some protection for such expression. For example, a Mississippi woman, a member of the African Hebrew Israelites church, wore a headwrap as part of her religious and cultural heritage. Her previous principal had permitted the headdress with no questions, but a new principal gave her written notice of "inappropriate dress." When she refused to stop wearing the headdress, the board of education discharged her, charging insubordination. Subsequently the court found that there was no evidence that the teacher's headdress had an adverse effect either on her ability to do her job or on the fulfillment of the school's educational mission.[7]

In conclusion, the "reasonableness" standard means that schools may enforce teacher dress codes when those codes represent a compelling interest related to the school's educational mission. Of course, this loose coupling also means that "reasonableness" is open to interpretation from jurisdiction to jurisdiction, depending on the effectiveness of the arguments in individual cases. A Connecticut court, for example, ruled that a school board was justified in requiring male educators to wear ties because the board presented the tie as a symbol of "professionalism" that was thus connected to the school's essential mission.[8] Another court struck down a dress code prohibiting women from wearing pantsuits, saying such attire does not impede the educational process and may even improve a teacher's performance, especially in preschool or elementary school.[9] In most cases, however, it is the employee who chooses a "nonstandard" personal appearance who has the burden of demonstrating that the dress code prohibiting that appearance is "so irrational that it may be branded arbitrary or the regulation will stand since personal appearance interests are less weighty than other liberty rights on the constitutional scale."[10]

Personal Life and Revealing Speech

Another aspect of conduct is the right to behave as one chooses in private. Privacy rights are not contained in the Constitution, but rather are construed from the First and, more often, the Fourteenth Amendments.

Because educators are placed in positions of trust, however, they often are held to standards in their private lives that other citizens may not be. This notion of public trust has allowed the courts, in some cases, to restrict "unconventional" behavior if such behavior is seen to be detrimental to the educational process.

Alexander and Alexander, in *American Public School Law*, discuss two aspects of privacy: 1) The right to determine how much personal information a person must reveal and 2) the freedom of individuals to do or not do certain acts or subject themselves to certain experiences. Most litigation on privacy rights involves issues of morality relating to sexual activity or use of marijuana or other illegal drugs.[11]

The courts have developed flexible rules that provide for balancing the public's interests in schools against the private interests of school employees. Thus the courts have upheld school boards in regulating personal conduct within presumably reasonable limits. However, when this presumption of "reasonableness" is challenged, litigation results and educators allege that school rules unreasonably invade their privacy.

Where do the community's interests begin and the school employee's right of privacy end? Two tests are involved:

1. Does the conduct directly affect the performance of the employee?
2. Has the conduct become the subject of such notoriety as to impair the capability to discharge the responsibility of the teaching position?

While the U.S. Supreme Court has not clearly defined the limits to be placed on teachers' and administrators' private lives, a number of cases at the High Court level and in lower courts have influenced judicial thought on educator privacy issues. In particular, issues involving sexual behaviors have been influential. Issues related to sexual misconduct and sexual harassment are taken up in Chapter Ten, but other, private, sexual conduct also has caused litigation.

Such cases can depend on how much personal freedom an individual abandons and reveals to other people. Court decisions vary on this topic, but the principle still prevails: Does the behavior significantly disrupt the education process or erode the teacher's credibility with students, colleagues, or parents? If the school district can show that the teacher has lost credibility, then the teacher may be fired.

For example, a single, female teacher was living with a "significant other," but administrators expressed their disapproval to the community and dismissed her for not being a role model to the students. In this case, *Thompson* v. *Southwest School District*, the teacher sued the district. The court found that until the district took action to suspend the teacher on grounds of immorality, people generally were unaware of the teacher's private life. The court decided that it was unfair for the board to make the issue public in order to get support for its position. The court found that the teacher's lifestyle had not interfered with her teaching ability, nor had it caused a disruption in the education process.[12]

However, what if the significant other was of the same sex?

Whether gay and lesbian teachers need legal protection from dismissal based on sexual orientation is a divisive and unsettled debate. Several states and some cities do have laws prohibiting sexual orientation discrimination in employment; however, even in those that do not, the principle remains the same: Is there a significant loss of credibility or disruption of the education process?

Court decisions about other behaviors have varied from state to state. Driving while intoxicated and smoking marijuana were found to be grounds for dismissal in one state but not in another, again depending of the degree of disruption of the education process.

Courts continually are asked to decide between a teacher's personal freedom and the community's rights to establish teacher behavior. At one time teachers could be fired for wearing lipstick, joining a certain church, or getting married. Now courts make a deliberate effort to balance the two sides. Each case must be judged on its own merit, but some trends have emerged.

Courts have agreed that a teacher can be fired for:

- Making public homosexual advances to non-students.
- Making sexual comments about a lesson in which the subject was not part of the curriculum.
- Engaging in sex with students.
- Inciting violence among students.
- Allowing students to drink alcohol.
- Drinking excessively.
- Using profanity and other abusive language to students.
- Having a sex change.
- Stealing school property.
- Not living in the district if it is listed as a condition for employment.

Courts have agreed that a teacher cannot be fired for:

- Obesity, unless it hampers performance.
- Private homosexual behavior.

- Smoking marijuana away from the school.
- Adultery.
- Use of vulgar language outside of school.
- AIDS or disability.

Courts have disagreed about whether a teacher can be fired for:

- Unwed cohabitation.
- Unwed parenthood.
- Conviction for shoplifting.

Freedom of Association

Finally, another expression of freedom is the joining of groups — freedom of association. The First Amendment gives individuals the right to peacefully assemble and petition. This guarantee of assembly means that educators, like other citizens, may associate with people or groups of their choosing. This is a freedom that sometimes is challenged, most notably in recent history during the Red Scare of the 1940s and 1950s.

The courts have determined that membership in an organization cannot be the basis for denying employment or for dismissal from employment. A 1947 New York decision, known as the Feinberg Law, was developed during a period of hysteria about communist infiltration into schools. That law ordered the New York Board of Regents to compile a list of subversive organizations that school people would not be allowed to join. Two decades later, in 1967, the Supreme Court declared such laws unconstitutional. This decision did not deny school boards the right to screen employees on various criteria but stated that membership in an organization was not ground for dismissal.[13]

Educators are permitted to actively participate in employee organizations or unions as long as such activity does not harm the educational process. Political activity also is permitted; employees have the right to vote, run for office, participate in campaigns, and speak out on public issues. Educators cannot be punished for social or political activism during nonschool hours.

However, problems can arise in establishing acceptable relationships between private actions and the ability to teach. There are different interpretations by different courts and school boards; a uniform law has been elusive. Thus educators must be aware that, as of this writing, no precise guidelines exist for balancing personal freedom in a political or social-action context with judgments about the effect of such freedom, when acted on, on an individual's professional competence.

Academic Freedom

Academic freedom concerns what is taught and how it is taught. Courts try to balance the right to academic freedom with the school system's right to see that its students are learning appropriate subject matter in an environment conducive to learning. If an issue is brought to the court, the judge looks to see if the activities are inappropriate, irrelevant to the subject as described in the syllabus, obscene, or substantially disruptive in discipline.

A 1998 case, *Lacks* v. *Ferguson Reorganized School District*,[14] illustrates the treatment that academic freedom gets in classrooms today. Veteran teacher Cecilia Lacks moved to a school system whose student body was 98% African American. Discouraged with their disinterest, she directed her students to write plays that reflected their lives. These plays contained many examples of vulgarity and profanity. After a student complained that the teacher had permitted the reading of a poem that had "profanity and graphic descriptions of oral sex," the principal charged her with failure to enforce the student code that prohibited profanity, and the board terminated her. The district court agreed with the teacher; but the decision was overturned on appeal.

Academic freedom for K-12 public school teachers is not what it used to be. People who analyze academic freedom cases have found that before 1980, teachers were as likely to win as school boards. During the 1980s, the trend turned, and teachers won only nine out of 17 academic freedom cases. Academic freedom certainly has a place in the school system, but administrators and school boards determine its exercise in appropriate circumstances.

Notes

1. Pickering v. Board of Education, 391 U.S. 563 (1968).
2. Tompkins v. Vickers, 26 F.3d 603 (5th Cir. 1994).
3. David Rubin, *The Rights of Teachers* (New York: Avon, 1972).
4. Case cited in Joel Spring, *American Education* (New York: McGraw-Hill, 1994), p. 273.
5. Tardif v. Quinn, 545 F.2d 761 (1st Cir. 1976).
6. Morrison v. Hamilton County Bd. of Educ., 494 S.W.2d 770 (Tenn. 1973), *cert. denied*, 414 U.S. 1044 (1974).
7. Mississippi Employment Security Comm'n v. McGlothin, 556 So. 2d 324 (Miss. 1990).
8. East Hartford Education Association v. Board of Education of the Town of East Hartford, 562 F.2d 838 (2d Cir. 1977).
9. *In re* School District of Kingley and Kingley Education Association, 56 Lab. Arb. 1138 (1971).
10. Kelley v. Johnson, 425 U.S. 238 (1976).
11. Kern Alexander and M. David Alexander, *American Public School Law* (St. Paul, Minn.: West, 1992).
12. Thompson v. Southwest School District, 483 F. Supp. 1170 (W.D.M.W.1980).
13. Elfbrandt v. Russell, 384 U.S. 11 (1966).
14. Lacks v. Ferguson Reorganized School District R-2, 936 F. Supp. 676 (E.D. Mo. 1996). Rehearing in 1998; Supreme Court refused to hear in 1999.

Chapter Three

PROFESSIONAL RESPONSIBILITY AND TORT LIABILITY

J ohn, a student, had a pit bull, a fighting dog, which he kept chained at his home. One day a friend of his decided to unchain the dog and take it to school. At the school, the dog bit another student, and the parents of the injured student sued the school district for negligence. Was the school responsible?

Consultant Carey E. Ferrell, speaking to a group of school board members at a Florida School Management Seminar, commented, "There is probably no aspect of school law that arouses as much interest or concern as that of tort liability." Yet educators, who daily are on the firing line, often are not aware of the responsibility and liability issues that form a basis for many torts.

What Is a Tort?

The first step in creating this awareness is to understand what a tort is. The word *tort* is derived from the Latin word *tortum*, or "twisted." The idea of "twisted" is applied to activity that deviates from accepted behavior. Thus a tort in legal parlance is an injury or wrongful action for which the legal system may provide a remedy.

Americans — indeed, citizens of most Western democracies — live in what has come to be called a "litigious society." Persons who have been wronged, or believe that they have been wronged, have the right to sue those who have wronged them and to recover damages in the form of monetary awards by the courts.

Because a tort is a civil wrong committed by a person against another person or that person's property with a resulting injury, the courts may provide monetary compensation if the injury (not necessarily physical) resulted from unreasonable conduct. State policies vary according to special immunities, liabilities, and related standards. However, general principles apply regardless of jurisdiction. Tort law developed as common law with judicial precedent having more predominance than statute.

Educators, like others who deal with the public and who hold a public trust, may be sued for willful or negligent actions. Legal suits against educators have increased, according to Nancy Haydon, a risk management supervisor in Marion County, Florida, because "1986 was an important year for torts in schools. This is the year when attorneys were deregulated and were permitted to advertise. When the lawyers come on television and tell you they will address your grievance, and you will not pay [the lawyer] unless you recover, people do not hesitate to sue."[1]

Parents (most often) are the ones who come to school looking to have a grievance addressed — and threatening to sue. Wendy Staley, an elementary principal, told me that teachers "just have no idea how many times I hear this [the threat to sue]." Often the threat can be turned aside by rational discussion. Says Staley, "I practice my best communication skills. First, I listen to them. I explain and discuss our point of view. Usually, we work it out right there, and it goes no farther."[2] But at other times no amount of discussion is sufficient to answer the grievance, and the aggrieved party brings suit.

The legal test for torts examines three areas:

- Existence of a legal duty. Did the defendant owe the plaintiff a duty?
- A breach of that duty. Did the defendant do or not do something with regard to the duty?

- A causal nexus, or connection, between the breach and the injury. Did the negligence cause the injury? The term *proximate cause* describes this relationship.

Classes of Torts

Tort liability falls into several areas; issues affecting education can be classified mainly as strict liability, intentional interference, or negligence. Negligence tends to be the area that most affects educators. Professional negligence, or educational malpractice, is a somewhat different issue and is taken up in the next chapter.

Strict liability involves intentional behavior by someone, such as a teacher, that causes harm. For example, a chemistry teacher stores two incompatible chemicals on the same shelf, and a student is injured when the two chemicals ignite. The teacher is liable because it was the teacher's responsibility to store the chemicals in a safe manner.

The standard of strict liability will not be imposed unless the activity is classified as "hazardous." However, hazards may be present in a wide variety of situations — in laboratory experiments with dangerous chemicals, in shop activities that use power saws, on field trips, or in the routine care of very young children. Teachers and administrators are liable for students' safety during fire emergencies. The definition of strict liability varies from state to state.

The courts also can invoke a liability standard if a person has been injured through no identifiable fault of anyone. In such cases, proving fault may not be necessary. In other words, the fact that an accident happened and an injury occurred can make one liable. Thus a person may be liable even though he or she is not strictly at fault for the other person's injury. In these kinds of cases, the courts still award damages based on the "strict liability" standard as applied to the defendant. This rule was adopted to place damages on the person best able to bear the burden. In these cases, the defendant's acts are not as important as the suffering of the injured person.

According to *The Restatement (Second) of Torts*, six factors determine whether an activity is abnormally dangerous:

- A high degree of risk of some harm to the person or property of others.
- Likelihood that the harm that results will be great.
- Inability to eliminate the risk by taking reasonable care.
- Extent to which the activity is not a matter of common usage.
- Inappropriateness of the activity for the place it is conducted.
- Extent to which its value to the community is outweighed by the dangerous attributes.[3]

The scenario at the start of this chapter, in which a student was injured by a dog, is similar to a 1992 case in Ohio, in which the parents sued the school, and not the dog owner, for negligence. The court ruled that the school district was not liable because the school's common law duty of care did not require constant supervision of school grounds, nor could the school officials have known that the dog was vicious and dangerous. If the parents had shown that the animal was abnormally dangerous, they possibly could have prevailed against the dog owner in a strict liability action.

While determining fault may not be necessary, the courts generally require that the defendant has "caused" some unusual hazard or abnormal danger — often simply by not removing or otherwise rendering harmless an existing hazard. This area of strict liability makes up a small element of the total tort picture in schools, but it is an area of litigation that appears to be growing.

Educators can guard against strict liability litigation by taking two actions. First, they should be certain to give clear and exact directions, including instruction in safety precautions, whenever a hazard is involved. Posting written warnings and safety instructions also can help to create awareness of potential hazards and thus minimize liability. Second, teachers, administrators, and other school people must ensure that equipment is maintained in good — nonhazardous — condition, that safeguards are intact and in place, and that safety equipment (goggles, fire blankets, etc.) is properly maintained and available.

Intentional interference is a tort liability that can involve teachers or administrators who unreasonably punish students. A Florida teacher taped an unruly kindergarten student's mouth shut, put him in a cardboard box, and tied him to a chair. The student fell over and hit his head. The parents sued. Not only did this incident — embellished by sensational press coverage — result in tort liability, but the action also resulted in the filing of child abuse charges.

Intentional interference torts occur when one person deliberately interferes with another, leading to harm. However, it is not necessary to establish intent to cause harm. While an action that causes injury may be voluntary, it is not necessarily hostile. A practical joke that causes injury is intentional interference.

David Splitt, writing in the *Executive Educator*, described the 1994 graduation at Gunn High School in Palo Alto, California, when a 65-pound smoke bomb "sprayed gobs of molten sugar and fertilizer across the surrounding campus." A number of students were hurt, including two girls who were severely burned. Splitt, whose article was published in 1996, emphasized that had the case not been settled out of court, the school district would have paid dearly. Attorneys accused the school administration of being too lenient in tolerating school pranks. When juries look at disfiguring injuries, they have little sympathy for the financial problems of a district. Splitt added, "Jurors are likely to agree [that] school officials should have foreseen the possibility of a tragedy since the administration had a track record of tolerating and even condoning senior pranks."[4]

Other examples of intentional interference include:

- False imprisonment: the intent to restrict the movement of a student. Reasonableness is a standard. For example, keeping a student after class or inside during recess is not false imprisonment, even if an injury occurs. The detention must be a reasonable response to some problem or infraction, and students who are kept after school must have a safe way to get home. However, false imprisonment can occur if a teacher or administrator confines a student for an unreasonable time or in a wrongful manner and an injury occurs. If a student is punished by being placed in a closet, for example, a subsequent injury might well be related to false imprisonment.

• Assault: when one is put in fear of harm by the actions of another. No physical contact is necessary, but the person who is assaulted is put in fear of physical harm. (Note: Criminal assault and battery are different from tort assault and battery.) Assault includes the threat of force through words or body posturing, an element of fear, and immediacy. A student's threat to "get" a teacher after school is not assault; nor is a student's threat to slash a teacher's car tires or ransack a teacher's or administrator's house.

• Battery: physical contact with another in a rude and angry manner. The absence of hostile intent does not preclude battery. Horseplay, practical jokes, pranks — all can be forms of battery. For example, a Maryland court ruled that a student who pulled a chair from under a teacher committed battery, though the action was meant as a joke.[5] On the other hand, a teacher or administrator can be charged with battery in the use of corporal punishment, regardless of its permissibility under the law, if the punishment is too severe or is unwarranted. Educators also can be liable in cases where one student batters another. One might ask, What is the teacher's duty when students fight? A teacher is not necessarily expected to intervene physically, particularly if such intervention might prove personally harmful. However, the teacher is obligated to tell the students to stop fighting, to send for help, and to render first aid.

• Defamation: slander (oral) or libel (written) that causes

ridicule or disrepute. When one person's reputation is injured by another's words, a defamation tort may be defined. The injury is to the esteem, respect, good will, or confidence of the injured person. People have a right to enjoy their reputations free from false or disparaging remarks. Defamation may be established by evidence that discloses previous ill will, hostility, threats, rivalry, previous libel and slander, or violence of language. In education settings defamation may involve statements about an individual's skills, qualifications, ethics, or other areas; and such statements must harm the individual in his or her pursuit of an education or profession. Defamatory statements must be untrue and result in an actual monetary loss for the defamed person.

- Intentional emotional distress: conduct that creates unreasonable emotional pain. An incident that offers an example involved an unruly fifth-grade student. The student was "clowning around" and so, to punish the student, the teacher took lipstick and made up the student's face as a clown. The student was forced to wear the clown makeup for the rest of the day.
- Trespass of personal property: unreasonable interference with property belonging to another person. School locker searches can fall into this category. This issue is taken up separately in Chapter Seven.

An example of intentional interference causing emotional distress involved a coach who played a trick on a kindergarten student. The student, Justin, and two of his friends were misbehaving during a rainy day movie, so the coaches had two of the boys sit with him. The boys started playing with his hair and ears, and the coach told them he would "kill them" if they did not stop. He took the two boys into his office while he did some paperwork, and the boys started interrogating the coach as to how he would kill them. The coach said he would tie a jump rope around their neck and push them off the chair. Then the coach asked the boys if they would like to play a trick on Justin by playing dead.

When Justin came into the office, he really believed the boys were dead.

After experiencing the "joke," Justin was diagnosed as having Post Traumatic Stress Disorder and had come to a realization that the world was not a safe place and that all adults could not be trusted. A psychiatrist testified that Justin had separation anxiety and social phobia disorder and would probably need three to five more years of therapy. After considering evidence from both sides, the court ruled that "this child has been effectively robbed of a normal, carefree childhood due to the careless actions of the coach." Monetary awards were given to the plaintiff.[6]

A few more words about defamation may be helpful. Many principals are concerned that teacher evaluations that are negative may lead to lawsuits on the basis of defamation. This is not the case. In fact, Perry Zirkel, in *The Law of Teacher Evaluation: A Self-Assessment Handbook*, points out that just the opposite may be true. Evaluation is one of the duties of a principal. The principal who fails to conduct proper evaluations of staff may be found to be negligent. Zirkel cites two cases in which appellate courts upheld the firing of principals who did not implement evaluation plans according to their school board's policies.[7]

Defamation claims by teachers have failed in states that grant absolute immunity for the evaluation process. In other states evaluation is within the duty of administrators, and no defamation can be claimed unless the plaintiff can prove that the administrator was acting out of malice.

Defamation must consist of untrue statements, either oral or in writing, that result in an actual loss of money. The major defenses against defamation suits are the truth of the statements and the absence of malice.

A related issue is so-called negligent hiring. For example, if a district knowingly hires a person who is not competent — or passes off a problem employee to another district by not providing an honest evaluation — then the original employer can be held liable if that employee (or former employee) subsequently behaves in a way that involves tort liability. A major question now being discussed among school attorneys involves liability related to known or suspected sex offenders who may be hired by a school district.

Negligence is defined as conduct that falls below an established standard of care and results in injury to a person. In other words, negligence can be found when a duty of care is established and a breach of that duty causes or results in injury. An important factor in establishing negligence is determining that the circumstances of injury were foreseeable and might have been avoided by prudent action or judgment. In an education setting the primary test of an acceptable standard of care consists in determining whether students are protected from unreasonable risks.

A 1994 case in Idaho illustrates an attempt to hold a teacher responsible for a student's injury on the basis of negligence. A teacher canceled his weightlifting class and, instead, held a softball game during which he supervised the students from behind the backstop. A student slid into first base and broke his ankle. The student claimed that the instructor was negligent in requiring them to play softball, failed to instruct students on how to play, and did not require proper footwear. The court determined, to the contrary, that the student failed to show a connection between the alleged negligence and the injury. No evidence was presented that the use of running shoes, rather than special baseball shoes, would have made a difference in avoiding injury. In other words, no relationship between the teacher's conduct and the student's injury could be established.[8]

Determination of negligence hinges on four elements: duty of care, standard of care, proximate or legal cause, and injury or actual loss.

1. Duty of Care. School teachers and administrators have a duty to provide a safe environment and to protect students from unreasonable risk of harm. If a situation is recognized as danger-

ous, then the responsible person — the teacher in the classroom, the teacher assigned to playground duty, and so on — has a duty to make the situation safe or to remove students from danger. However, risks can arise suddenly. The courts generally have ruled that no duty of care exists where the responsible persons could not reasonably have foreseen the danger.

In the Introduction to this book I described a case in which a teacher's aide was charged with negligence when a seven-year-old boy was blinded after being struck by a rock thrown by another student. The Supreme Court of Wyoming determined that the teacher's aide was not negligent in this case. The teacher's aide could not reasonably be expected to anticipate that a student would throw a rock at another student. Indeed, this 1972 case points up a principle of negligence that is particularly germane in education settings: Reasonable supervision does not require constant scrutiny. Nor was the school found at fault because a rock was present on the playground. Responding to this latter charge of negligence, the court stated that "left on the ground, a rock could hurt no one."[9]

2. Standard of Care. A standard of care is defined by the care a reasonable and prudent person might exercise under given circumstances. In determining "reasonable and prudent," the court will decide what oversight or action should be taken to prevent injury and then determine whether that oversight or action was taken in the case presented to it. The standard of care will vary according to the circumstances. For example, a reasonable person would know that children doing a science experiment need closer supervision than do children who are reading quietly.

In 1976 the Illinois Supreme Court ruled on a case that has set a general standard. A 13-year-old girl suffered spinal injuries when she fell while trying to hang from her knees on steel rings suspended from the ceiling. The girl contended that the gymnastics teacher failed to provide proper instruction and supervision. The court ruled that the plaintiffs who sued on behalf of the girl "had failed to prove that the defendants were guilty of willful and wanton misconduct."[10] In other words, the teacher did exercise a sufficient standard of care, even though the student was subsequently injured. The phrase "willful and wanton misconduct" is an important concept.

To illustrate further, in 1978 a court faced a case in which a kindergarten pupil was burned when a pot of boiling water fell on the student during class. The parents claimed that the teacher was guilty of "willful and wanton misconduct" by allowing the child to play under the table that held the water. However, the court found no evidence of misconduct. The decision was appealed, and the appellate court ruled that while some negligence possibly existed, teachers (in Illinois) are not subject to greater liability than are parents.[11] This is a useful rule of thumb that echoes the long-implicit, sometimes explicit standard of *in loco parentis* — that is, that teachers (and other school personnel) act in the place of parents as responsible caregivers.

A Nebraska music teacher taught her first-grade class to play "London Bridge," a game in which two students link arms and swing a third student back and forth. She started the music and started writing on the board. During the game, a student was thrown into a bookcase and was cut above the eyebrow. The student contended that he told the other students three times to stop and that he called for help. He required 50 stitches and had headaches and blurred vision. The court held that the teacher's failure to directly supervise the early portion of the students' first game of London Bridge constituted negligence and awarded the student more than $21,000. On appeal, the district argued that the trial court had held the teacher to a higher standard of legal responsibility than was appropriate for first-graders. However, the appellate court agreed that not applying a standard of care at the beginning of the game and failure to stop the aggressive swinging of the other students was negligent and caused the injury. The plaintiff won.[12]

When negligence is established, the question becomes, Who pays? Although the doctrine of government immunity is slowly eroding, some states have waived immunity to the amount of insurance coverage. For example, in 1973 the Florida Legislature enacted a comprehensive law waiving sovereign immunity of the state and all its agencies and subdivisions. The law authorizes suits against agencies, including school boards, to recover damages in tort for injury, loss of property, or death caused by negligent or wrongful act or omission of employees while in the scope of their office. Public agencies are liable for tort claims just as private citizens are, except the liability does not include punitive damages or interest for the periods prior to the judgment. The liability is limited to $100,000 on any single claim or judgment and a total of $200,000 for all claims. A school board is not responsible for amounts in excess of these limits.

Florida also implemented a "hold harmless" provision, which means a person cannot be held personally liable unless that individual acted in bad faith, with malice, or with disregard for human rights. This provision and similar acts in other states are very important for teachers and other school employees.

As risk increases, so does the standard of care. This has some bearing on supervision of students. "Reasonableness" changes with age. Children up to the age of seven cannot be held liable for negligence, thus teachers must be more vigilant in situations that pose a danger of injury. Children older than seven may be judged to be negligent, depending on the circumstances. Thus, in the incident of the student being blinded by another student throwing a rock, the rock-thrower's legal liability would depend to some extent on his or her age. The older the thrower, the more likely that he or she could reasonably be expected to understand that rock-throwing is dangerous.

3. Proximate or Legal Cause. "Cause" is the connection between an act and a resulting injury. Did a teacher's negligent conduct lead to a pupil's injury? Note, however, that the teacher's conduct does not have to be the direct cause of injury. A teacher — for example, a playground supervisor — might be judged to be negligent if a student is hit by a baseball during an unsupervised melee that might have been prevented by reasonable super-

vision. In such a case the teacher could be found negligent even though the teacher did not throw the ball that hit the student.

4. Injury or Actual Loss. Some real injury must occur in order for damages to be awarded in cases of negligence. For example, damages might be assessed to pay for medical bills of an injured student or for subsequent special tutoring in the event that the student was unable to return to his or her regular school.

Paraprofessionals and Others in the School

Aides, interns, and other paraprofessionals must meet the standard of care that a teacher would be held to in the same or similar circumstances. Therefore solid training is a necessary preventative for legal problems involving paraprofessional duties.

Teachers are held to a higher standard of care for the supervision and safety of young people in their charge than the person on the street would be. If a child runs into the street and is hit by a car, an adult bystander who might (or might not) have prevented the accident is not responsible. If a teacher and students are walking along a street and a student dashes out and is struck, the teacher probably will be seen as responsible — because it is the teacher's job to care for the children. Such care is not a bystander's job.

Woodrow Clymer, director of employee relations in Marion County, Florida, said in an interview, "I am always amazed that adults make such inappropriate decisions." Clymer's job is to mediate grievances and investigate situations that have escalated into major problems. "Principals, teachers, and paraprofessionals alike can do some very stupid things — without thinking."[13]

A standard of care similar to that of teachers is expected for those who assist or substitute for teachers; however, liability is shared because teachers and administrators also are responsible for informing and training paraprofessionals and others who work in the school setting. This extends to cafeteria workers, custodians, secretaries, and other school employees in most cases.

Volunteers also fall into this category. James Harshfield, writing in the *Bulletin* of the National Association of Secondary School Principals, noted that school leaders must do the following in order to limit tort liability connected to the use of parent and community volunteers:

- Develop relevant policies and procedures to manage volunteers.
- Maintain adequate and appropriate liability insurance.
- Develop descriptions of responsibilities for volunteers.
- Sufficiently screen volunteers.
- Provide orientation and training for volunteers.
- Adequately supervise volunteers.[14]

These are effective principles to extend to all staff. The use of these solid, risk-management strategies will lower the potential for negligent acts and subsequent legal actions against a district or individual school employees or volunteers.

Protections Against Lawsuits

When it comes to protecting schools and educators from lawsuits, as one attorney I know says, "The best protection is a caring, responsive staff." When there is a problem, a positive, understanding attitude coupled with good communication can solve many seemingly impossible problems. Two of the most important principles to remember are:

1. Provide consistent, reasonable care, always looking ahead to possible problems.
2. Act as a prudent, conscientious parent would act in a similar situation.

Several forms of defense are available in lawsuits arising out of the school setting: governmental immunity, assumption of risk, contributory negligence, comparative negligence, and act of God.

Governmental, or Sovereign, Immunity. This defense means the state, federal, or local government agencies are immune from suit and cannot be held responsible. This stance means that if a person is injured as a result of an educator's negligence, that individual's only recourse is against the educator who was negligent. The school district is immune from suit unless the state has given permission for citizens to sue the district, thereby waiving immunity.

This defense is called sovereign: "The king can do no wrong." Governmental immunity exempts school districts from liability and tort damages, but it does not protect individuals; teachers and administrators can be sued.

Some states have changed this stance; others still maintain sovereign immunity for school districts. Some states have waived immunity through "save harmless" statutes to a point where most injuries can be compensated. The Illinois Supreme Court in striking down sovereign immunity reasoned, "It is almost incredible that in this modern age of. . . enlightenment, . . . the medieval absolutism supposed to be implicit in . . . 'the King can do no wrong,' should exempt the various branches of the government from liability."[15]

As might be supposed, this area of the law is complex, and individual jurisdictional laws are changing constantly. The best way to keep up with these changes is to keep an eye on current legislation and, when a problem arises, to consult an attorney. Clearly, one safeguard for individuals is to carry liability insurance, which is available through education organizations and many homeowner's policies.

Assumption of Risk. This defense is used in cases where an individual chooses to participate in a risky activity with full knowledge of the risks involved. Schools that sponsor sports often fall back on this defense when a student player is injured. But the defense also has been extended to sports instructors and supervisors and spectators. For example, a teacher's aide was struck in the head by a volleyball during a game of "warball." The court ruled the aide knew how the game was played. A student missed the target and hit the aide. The court ruled that a participant has no duty not to accidentally injure a spectator, who is fully aware of the risks.[16]

The courts will consider the age, intelligence, and experience of the participants and the presence of warnings. Proper instruction (or lack of instruction) can influence the court's decision. For example, there are inherent risks in playing baseball; however, if a student has not been taught to drop the bat after hitting a pitched ball and, instead, tosses it and strikes another player, then the teacher may be liable for improper instruction.

Contributory Negligence. This defense is used to claim that a plaintiff's own negligence caused the injury. The plaintiff's conduct fell below the standard which would protect the individual. If the court finds the plaintiff's own actions are negligent, the person may not recover damages. Some states do not allow this defense.

When contributory negligence is used in actions involving injury to students, the student is held to a standard of care that is reasonable and prudent for a student of similar age in similar circumstances, taking into account experience, training, education, and maturity. For example, a Tennessee court found contributory negligence when a 12-year-old died from head injuries that he received when his head struck a utility pole while he was leaning out of the window of a moving school bus. The court ruled the student's own actions were the proximate cause, because all students had been warned not to put any part of their body outside the window. The boy had been an intelligent and excellent student.[17] Clearly, this defense cannot be used in cases that involve very young students.

Comparative Negligence. This defense is viable when it can be shown that an injury was partly the fault of several persons. Some states apportion damages according to the assessed degrees of fault of the parties. For example, a jury may find that a running student who tripped over a mop left by a custodian is 40% negligent, and the custodian who left the mop is 60% negligent. Thus if the awarded damages are $10,000, the student will recover $6,000. In some states, plaintiffs may not recover damages if their level of negligence is 50% or more.

Act of God. This defense is useful when an accident occurs that cannot be foreseen. If a school had an old, weak, or poorly constructed flagpole that breaks during a high wind and injures a student, then liability would be imposed on the school for negligence. On the other hand, if a bolt of lightning strikes a properly constructed pole causing it to break and injure a student, then no liability would be imposed on the school because the proximate cause was an "act of God."

Insurance

In many states the defense of governmental immunity will be waived to the extent that the district has purchased insurance coverage. Some districts are forming their own corporations and self-insuring. Courts generally have held schools or their agents liable for injuries sustained during the course of regular school events that result from failure to provide a reasonably safe environment, failure to warn participants of known hazards (or to remove known dangers wherever possible), failure to properly instruct students in an activity, or failure to provide adequate supervision for an activity.

Individual educators should be aware of four types of insurance:

1. *Tort liability insurance,* which can be issued by unions and professional associations, may be useful in instances when the school district's liability insurance would not be available, as in cases of sexual misconduct or sexual harassment. This type of insurance sometimes can be added to a homeowner's policy.

2. *Malpractice insurance* may be available from some of the same sources as tort liability insurance. While physician's mal-

practice insurance is a major investment for doctors, educator's malpractice insurance is considerably less expensive. The reason is fairly simple: In teaching, the standards of practice are hard to define. Generally the courts have taken the position that a teacher must provide the opportunity to learn but cannot be responsible for a student's failure to learn. The courts recognize that there are circumstances over which the teacher has no control.

3. *Automobile insurance,* preferably provided by the school district, is essential for anyone who transports students as a part of his or her job. Most personal automobile coverage is too limited to provide adequate protection for those who must routinely transport students to cheerleading conferences, interschool debates, and other off-premises school activities.

4. *Personal property insurance* also is a must for teachers who plan to use their own property — computer, videotape player, stereo — at school. The laptop computer that disappears because a custodian leaves the classroom door unlocked while a school dance is held in the building can be an expensive loss for the unprotected teacher. Some homeowner's policies cover possessions taken or kept outside the home; other policies permit a rider to be added for that purpose.

Notes

1. Interview with Nancy Haydon, risk management supervisor, Marion County, Florida, 5 April 1997.
2. Interview with Wendy Staley, principal, Maplewood Elementary School, Ocala, Florida, 21 March 1997.
3. *Restatement (Second) of Torts* (St. Paul, Minn.: West, 1984), section 20, p. 20.
4. David Splitt, "Don't Let the Last Laugh Be on You," *Executive Educator* 18 (June 1996): 11.
5. Ghassemick v. Schafer, 447 A.2d 84 (Md. 1982).
6. Spears v. Jefferson Parish School Board, 646 So. 2d 1104 (Court of Appeals of Louisiana, 1994).
7. Perry Zirkel, *The Law of Teacher Evaluation: A Self-Assessment Handbook* (Bloomington, Ind.: Phi Delta Kappa Educational Foundation, 1996).
8. Sanders v. Kana Joint School Dist., 876 P.2d 154 (Idaho App. 1994).
9. Fagan v. Summers, 498 P.2d 1227 (1972).

10. Koblyanski v. Chicago Board of Education, 347 N.E.2d 705 (1976).
11. McCauley v. Chicago Board of Education, 384 N.E.2d 100 (1978).
12. Johnson v. District of Millard, 253 Neb. 634, 573 N.W.2d 116 (1998).
13. Interview with Woodrow Clymer, director of employee relations, Marion County School Board, 14 October 2005.
14. James B. Harshfield, "Liability Issues of Using School Volunteers in Public Schools." *NASSP Bulletin* (September 1996): 65.
15. Molitor v. Kaneland Community Unit Dist. No. 302, 163 N.E.2d 89 (1959) at 94-96.
16. Melder v. State Farm Fire & Casualty Co., 498 So. 2d 1095 (La. Ct. App. 1986).
17. Arnold v. Hayslett, 655 S.W.2d 941 (Tenn. 1983).

Chapter Four

CLASSROOM ORGANIZATION AND MANAGEMENT

The law holds, in general, that educators are professionals with the ability to make organizational and managerial decisions. This is broadly stated, and so some issues related to organizational and managerial decisions are necessarily addressed in other sections of this book. In this chapter I will focus on classroom organization and management issues, which relate primarily to classroom teachers, rather than specialist teachers or other school employees. Administrators are involved in these issues as supervisors of teachers.

In practice, a wide variety of issues falls under this dual heading, including organizational issues (ability grouping, or tracking; promotion and retention; and fees for educational services), management issues (incompetence, insubordination, misuse of sick leave), and educational malpractice issues.

Organizational Issues

Ability Grouping, or Tracking. Not long ago I presented a Socratic seminar on ability grouping to a class of Saint Leo University students. The students used two journal articles — one supported tracking, one supported heterogeneous grouping. After the discussion, a student confessed, "I thought I knew what I believed, now I'm not sure." To track or not to track; that's the dilemma. Research results are as mixed as students' feelings about the subject. But what do the courts say?

Basically, the courts have said that ability grouping is a matter of educational choice. Only when that choice can be shown to have negative effects can the practice of ability grouping, or tracking, be called into question legally. For example, in 1984 the Eleventh Court of Appeals held that ability grouping is a question only when the resulting groups are racially disproportionate.[1] Even then, grouping may be permitted if the groups do not perpetuate segregation. However, in multiracial circumstances, the courts may favor limited groups, such as homogeneous reading or math classes, with other classes being heterogeneously grouped. It should be noted that, in 1985, the same court held that ability grouping, in fact, may provide better educational opportunities than heterogeneous grouping for minorities in some circumstances.[2]

Promotion and Retention. Another classroom management issue that may cause concern is student promotion and retention. The courts have made it clear that student assignment — whether a student is promoted from one grade to the next or retained in grade for a second year — is within the discretion of the local school board. Local school boards are permitted to use such factors as a student's age, intelligence, ability, and training as criteria to make a promotion/retention decision. Parents have few grounds on which to object, and the courts usually have chosen not to intervene in local decisions.

A case in point: A second-grade teacher failed 22 out of 23 students because they did not meet the standards established for a reading program. The plaintiffs (the children's parents) said they knew that the students did not complete the required work but claimed that the children were capable of doing third-grade work anyway. They accused the teacher of being negligent and careless in the supervision of instruction. The court disagreed and ruled for the teacher.[3] Denial of promotion for failure to complete reasonable requirements does not violate a student's rights.

Another case, *Debra P. v. Turlington,*[4] has ramifications for today's high-stakes testing movement. Florida had enacted that passing a minimum competence test was a requirement for graduation. Debra P. challenged the law and argued that a diploma, a property right, had been denied although the state could not show that the public school curriculum had prepared the students for the test. The court recognized the importance to the future welfare of individuals to have a high school diploma.

Declaring the issue to be the validity of the test, the Fifth Circuit remanded the case for further findings to determine whether the literacy test covered materials taught in Florida's classrooms. The Department of Education went to every school in the state and gathered evidence that the basic questions were being covered and presented the massive document to the court. The court then accepted the material as valid and ruled for the state.

This ruling has been used by other courts to look at tests and probably will be used in the future for other challenges. The decision demands that tests do what they are supposed to do: measure what has been taught. The decision established quantitative measures for the state to show that tests are a fair assessment.

Courts generally have ruled that grades cannot be reduced as a disciplinary measure for violation of school rules. A Pennsylvania case illustrates this point. A student, while on a school field trip, drank a glass of wine in violation of school rules. The school suspended her from cheerleading, the National Honor Society, and all school activities and imposed a penalty of grade reduction for the days she was out of school. The board policy called for a reduction of grades in all classes for each day she was out of school. The court ruled for the student and held that the school board may not impose a grade reduction for infractions that are not related to education. To do this is to misrepresent the student's true scholastic achievement for college entrance and other purposes.[5]

Fees for Educational Services. When school budgets are tight, the number of cases related to charging fees for various education-related services tends to rise. Perhaps that is because the imposition of such fees also tends to increase during tight times. The courts often split on whether certain fees are legal and legitimate, usually depending on how the state constitution is written. If the constitution says that education is to be provided simply "without tuition," the courts generally have ruled that various fees are permissible. On the other hand, if the constitution says that the state is to "provide free education for all," the courts are more likely to take a negative view of any added fees.

Examples show this contrast. In 1984 the California Supreme Court decided that a district may not charge fees for dramatic productions, musical performance, and athletics participation.[6] But the next year a Michigan court upheld an athletic fee, saying that the fee was legitimate because the athletic program was not part of the regular educational program.[7]

Management Issues

Three areas come immediately to mind in terms of management: incompetence, insubordination, and misuse of sick leave. The first of these, incompetence, is perhaps the most often alleged.

Incompetence. Although incompetence can be included in several sections of this book, I take it up here because incompetence in terms of classroom management often is the first area in which this issue arises. The courts have given incompetence a broad interpretation: "want of physical, intellectual, or moral ability; insufficiency; inadequacy; specific want of legal qualifications or fitnesses."[8] But incompetence also is a political catchword. Not long ago the Florida legislature discussed doing away with teacher tenure in order to make it easier to get rid of "incompetent" teachers.

While the interpretation of incompetence has been broadly cast, incompetence seldom is dealt with only in general terms. Teachers who are alleged to be incompetent may be subject to numerous charges, for example, lack of subject-matter knowledge, lack of classroom discipline, unreasonable discipline, or willful neglect of duty. An apt illustration is the case of an Iowa teacher who was dismissed on the basis of 14 areas of incompetence, including poor discipline, excessive use of films, ineffective teaching, and failure to cooperate with administrators. The court upheld the teacher's dismissal.[9]

The state's issuance of a teaching license (or certificate) carries an assumption of competence. Therefore, in cases of incompetence, the school board must bear the burden of proof. Such was the case in Florida, where a certified teacher with 25 years experience was dismissed because the school board was able to demonstrate that the teacher used poor grammar and made spelling errors. She also attempted to teach spelling before the children mastered the alphabet.[10]

General lack of order and method can lead to charges of incompetence. A Philadelphia teacher was dismissed because she could not maintain order in the classroom. The room was cluttered with paper, "junk," and sunflower seeds. The furniture and walls were covered with graffiti. She also failed to give her students proper directions and did not plan her lessons.[11]

Some states require that school officials provide remedial training to staff who are alleged to be incompetent. If the statutes require such remediation, then the school board must prove that remediation was attempted but that the situation did not improve in order to convince state officials that incompetence is a valid reason for dismissal. A Missouri school district fired a teacher with 17 years experience after she failed to comply with specific recommendations to improve her performance. The teacher complained that previous evaluations showed her to be competent and that the district deliberately put her in classes with difficult students that could not be managed. However, the appellate court upheld the firing, noting that the teacher had, indeed, failed to comply with the school district's remedial recommendations and that there was no evidence that the district had engineered the classes against her.[12]

Inappropriate instruction can be construed as incompetence. A tenured Louisiana junior high teacher showed a portion of a horror movie, *Child's Play*, to a reading class. There was no discussion of the movie, which was not a regular part of the curriculum. The school district fired the teacher. Later, the court determined that the foul language and violent scenes in the movie sufficiently documented that the teacher willfully neglected her instructional duty to choose appropriate instructional materials and that the teacher demonstrated incompetence by showing a film with no educational value.[13]

Inappropriate punishment of students also can lead to a charge of incompetence. A principal tied a five-year-old kindergartner to a desk with rope and duct tape and placed him in the doorway of her office. Several employees observed the student crying for two hours before he was returned to class. The school board demoted the principal for incompetence. A Louisiana appeals court later also ruled that she was incompetent and affirmed the decision to demote her.[14]

Educators define incompetence in terms of poor work performance, while the courts may define it as the lack of ability, the lack of such legal qualifications as certification, or the lack of fitness to discharge the required duties. Dismissal for incompetence is based on a pattern or a number of factors, rather than on one single incident or event. The principal needs to follow the NEAT procedure: Notice, Expectations, Assistance, and Time to implement the suggested changes. Incompetence is difficult to prove and must be fully documented to withstand a challenge.

The National School Board's *A School Law Primer* suggests the following practices to help establish effective evaluation procedures:

1. Set standards and expectations with an evaluation document that enumerates specific behaviors that the evaluator can observe.
2. Apply all procedures and standards equally to all teachers. For example, never negatively evaluate a teacher for failure to turn in lesson plans on time when other teachers do not receive negative evaluations for the same behavior. This

will lead the teacher to correctly claim he or she has been treated unfairly.

3. Evaluations must be a candid, realistic assessment of the teacher and point out weaknesses and problems. Do not give artificially high ratings, for they may complicate future employment decisions.

4. Written evaluations must be specific. Give the facts on which conclusions are made. For example, do not just say the teacher's classroom is disorderly; give specific examples. Do not just say "needs improvement," but give a narrative of the situation and suggest videos, books, or other strategies that may help. The directives for improvement should be reasonable and provide ample time for improvement.

5. Personally observe the teacher on several occasions and in different settings. If in the classroom, remain an entire period. Have more than one person observe the teacher; this will avoid personality conflicts.

6. Refer to any previous discussion and evaluations; describe progress or lack of progress.

7. The evaluation should put the teacher on notice that there may be consequences if improvements are not made.

8. Avoid inflammatory statements, such as "I thought you were smarter than that."

9. Meet with the teacher and lay out the expectations and evaluation. Give the teacher an opportunity to challenge the opinions and observations.

10. Provide the teacher with a copy of the evaluation.

11. Extensive follow up of a teacher's job performance is required if deficiencies were noted in the evaluation.[15]

Insubordination. The courts have defined insubordination as a "willful disregard of expressed or implied directions of the employer and a refusal to obey reasonable orders."[16] For insubordinate behavior to be proved, conduct must be documented as violating a pertinent, reasonable school rule or order. Also, neither the rule nor actions taken to enforce it can be based on bias or discrimination or violate First Amendment rights, especially as applied to free speech or academic freedom.

Many cases of insubordination involve teachers willfully doing something they were told not to do. On the other hand, teachers also have been dismissed for not doing something, such as for being absent from an assigned duty station or failing to attend required meetings.

In the first category, a Kansas teacher requested leave to go to a job interview in Texas during the last week of school. The request was denied. The teacher called in sick and went anyway. Later, the principal from Texas called for a recommendation for the teacher, which confirmed the teacher's unauthorized conduct. The teacher was fired for insubordination. The courts agreed that this conduct was insubordinate and therefore unacceptable.[17]

Misuse of sick leave. Related in theme to the previous illustration is the next example. A Pennsylvania couple planned a ski trip to Colorado for a week in February. Their request for four days of personal leave was denied. The local teacher association filed a grievance on the couple's behalf, which the superintendent also denied. The couple went anyway. When they returned, they presented letters from a clinical psychologist, who said that they needed a temporary leave of absence from work. The school board did not agree. Legal action followed, and the board appealed to the state trial court, which stated that the couple's action was a misuse of sick leave. The appellate court ruled for the board, characterizing the teachers' actions "as lying or making false statements to a district administrator and was persistent and willful violation of school law."[18]

Educational Malpractice

The first major educational malpractice case was tried in California in the mid-1970s. A California statute requires graduates to read at an eighth-grade level. A student, Peter W., graduated from a San Francisco high school unable to read at this level. He sued the school on five counts of negligence and carelessness, claiming malpractice. However, eventually the court of appeals dismissed the case.[19] Indeed, claims of educational malpractice generally have failed because the courts are hesitant to interfere with school operations.

Some other examples further illustrate this area of litigation. In New York a student had a very difficult time in his classes but scored well on standardized tests. Because of his test scores, he was placed in a regular class. When he entered high school, he was reclassified as "learning disabled." Subsequently the student sued, claiming that the district was guilty of educational malpractice for not placing him properly. He also accused the elementary school principal of altering test results so that the school would "look good." This grade alteration, the student alleged, also denied him access to special programs. The appellate court said that New York did not recognize malpractice as a legal cause of action and dismissed that part of the case. However, the court also told the student that if he could produce evidence that the principal had changed the grades, then the court would consider that question.[20]

In another case a second-grade student in Michigan hanged himself after viewing a film called *Nobody's Useless*. In the film, a young disabled boy attempts suicide; but after the failed attempt, he learns to overcome his disability. The student's estate sued the district, the school board, and the superintendent for educational malpractice because of the showing of the film. Later, the appeals court affirmed that the board's showing the film to a second-grade class was a choice that it was empowered to make.[21]

While these are only a few examples, the point is that issues of educational malpractice have thus far been blunted. However, there always is a possibility that a strong case may appear that will have different results and may begin an avalanche of educational malpractice cases.

Notes

1. Bester v. Tuscaloosa City Board of Education, 722 F.2d 1514 (11th Cir. 1984).
2. Georgia State Conference of Branches of NAACP v. State of Georgia, 775 F.2d 1403 (11th Cir. 1985).
3. Sandlin v. Johnson, 643 F.2d 1027 (4th Cir. 1981).
4. Debra P. v. Turlington, 564 F. Supp. 177 (M.D. Fla., 1983) 564 F. Supp. 177; *aff'd*, 730 F.2d 1405 (11th Cir. 1984).
5. Katzman v. Cumberland Valley School District, 84 Pa. Cmwlth. 474, 479 A.2d.671 (1984).
6. Hartzell v. Connell, 679 P.2d 35 (Cal. 1984).
7. Attorney General v. East Jackson Public School, 372 N.W.2d 638 (Mich. App. 1985).
8. Beilan v. Board of Education, 357 U.S. 399 (1958).
9. Board of Directors of Sioux City v. Mroz, 295 N.W.2d 447 (Iowa 1980).
10. Blunt v. Marion County School Board, 515 F.2d 951 (5th Cir. 1975).
11. Board of Educ. of Sch. Dist. of Philadelphia v. Kerschner, 109 Pa. Cmwlth. 120, 530 A.2d 541 (Pa. 1987).
12. Newcomb v. Humansville R-IV School Dist., 908 S.W.2d 821 (Mo. App. S.D. 1995).
13. Roberts v. Rapides Parish School Board, 617 So. 2d 187 (La. App. 3d Cir. 1993).
14. Sylvester v. Cancienne, 664 So. 2d 1259 (La. App. 1st Cir. 1995).
15. National School Boards Association and Council of School Attorneys, *A School Law Primer, Part I* (Alexandria, Va., 1999).
16. School District No. 8, Pinal County v. Superior Court, 102 Ariz. 478, 433 P.2d 28 (1967).
17. Gaylord v. Bd. of Educ., School Distr. 218, 794 P.2d 307 (Kan. App. 1990).
18. Riverview Sch. Dist. v. Riverside Educ. Assoc., 639 A.2d 974 (Pa. Commnw. 1994).
19. Peter W. v. San Francisco Unified School District, 60 Cal. App. 3d 814 (1976).
20. Helbig v. City of New York, 622 N.Y.S.2d 316 (N.Y. App. Div. 1995).
21. Nalepa v. Plymouth-Canton Community Sch. Dist., 525 N.W.2d 897 (Mich. App. 1994).

Chapter Five

CURRICULUM, CENSORSHIP, AND COPYRIGHT

Schools are, by their very nature, "marketplaces" of ideas. Teachers and students function most effectively when that marketplace is least constrained or, rather, constrained only within the limitations of the First Amendment and related statutes.

Idea marketplace problems arise most often in the area of curriculum — the question of what should be taught — and, within that area, involve censorship and copyright issues. School boards have the power to determine local curricula. They may require that certain subjects or topics be taught, and they can determine that other subjects or topics will not be taught. The courts have been hesitant to intervene in curricular matters of a general nature.

For example, what happens if the school requires a certain class but a student's parents refuse to allow the student to take that class? Very early on — in 1878, as a matter of fact — a court case established the principle that if the student refuses to take a required course, the school has the right to expel the student. In this particular case, a girl decided not to take algebra because her father told her not to.[1]

However, there are exceptions to this principle. For example, if the refusal to take a class is based on a religious objection, the school may not be able to force the issue. The same can be true in cases involving other constitutional rights. However, in some instances the religion argument can be blunted by a reasonable accommodation. A 1962 case in Alabama may be illustrative. A girl contended that she should not be required to take physical education because she believed that the standard physical education attire that the district required was immodest, and she objected to some of the exercises. She also said that she did not want to be around other girls dressed in a "sinful" manner. The school board proposed that the girl could choose her dress and exercises. In subsequent legal action the court ruled that the board had made allowances in accommodating her dress and activity and, therefore, could require the girl to take physical education. The court decided that requiring the girl to attend the class did not violate her constitutional rights.[2]

Curriculum Issues

Several general issues relating to curriculum are academic freedom, sex education, evolution, community service, and animals in the classroom. In some cases these issues also involve censorship questions, but I will include a separate section on censorship later. The last part of this chapter deals with copyright matters.

Academic Freedom. In Chapter Two, we looked at academic freedom from the point of view of teacher rights. Here we consider academic freedom in terms of curriculum and classroom teaching. Freedom of speech within the classroom usually is construed as the right of a teacher to determine the specific subject matter and methods that best serve the instructional purposes of the class. This is "academic freedom," the freedom to make curricular and instructional choices without undue interference or restraints from administrators or the government. A teacher generally is protected from dismissal for exercising this freedom — unless the teacher violates a specific school board policy or a specific law.

In the famous *Tinker* decision of 1969, the U.S. Supreme Court provided the test for free speech as it applies to students and educators:

Freedom of speech may be restricted only where it substantially interferes with the requirements of the maintenance of order and discipline in the operation of the school or the furtherance of the educational process through balanced and relevant presentations.[3]

Does this mean that teachers can teach whatever they want or use whatever materials come to hand? Of course not. Curricular choices must be made on the following bases:

- Teachers' statements or materials must serve a valid educational purpose.
- Local school boards have the right and the responsibility to establish curricula, select textbooks, and prescribe general course content.
- The teacher must be responsible for choosing instructional methods and specific content within the bounds established by the board.

With the advent of state standards and requirements, some teachers claim they now are being required to teach to the test. The standards are general guidelines about what the state expects to be taught and the high-stakes tests will assess learning based on these standards. Teachers still have latitude in the selection, method, and presentation of material.

If a teacher uses the classroom to expound personal political views or other ideas that are irrelevant to the subject being taught, he or she may be disciplined. For example, a math teacher teaching Pythagorean theorem would have a hard time connecting it to a discussion of abortion.

This is not to say that teachers may not deal with controversial issues. However, controversial issues must be dealt with by taking into account the age, intelligence, and experience of the students, in addition to the manner in which any controversial content is connected to or integral to the curriculum. Balancing viewpoints also is a consideration.

What about offensive language? In one case an English teacher was fired for using the word *fuck* in a lecture on taboos and socially unacceptable words. Subsequently, the court ordered her reinstatement but noted that if the board of education had had specific guidelines about the language to be used in classroom discussions, then the firing probably would have been upheld.[4] In this case the offending word was integral to the discussion. But it should be clear that language (like other conduct) that is unnecessary and inappropriate is not protected. Offensive speech, such as the use of obscenities or vulgarity, usually is not construed as protected in the education setting.

Curricular choices that do not meet acceptable standards for instruction also are suspect. A 1987 court decision in Kentucky upheld a teacher's dismissal for showing an objectionable film that also was simply a time-filler with no related instructional purpose. The teacher showed *Pink Floyd — The Wall*, an "R" rated film, while she completed report cards on the last day of school. She had not previewed the film, nor did she discuss it in any way with the students. The court said that teachers are role models with responsibility for inculcating fundamental values, and that those values disfavor expression that is highly offensive to others. It ruled that the teacher's conduct was not protected by academic freedom because the film served no educational purpose. Also, because the teacher was out of the room while the film was shown, it did not even qualify as expression that could be protected by the First Amendment.[5]

Since the 1970s, many cases relating to content and methods have been filed. However, the Supreme Court seems deeply committed to allowing educators the freedom to act as true professionals.

Sex Education. Seemingly "extreme" cases of sex education involving condom demonstrations and condom distribution have made headlines, but sex education that is conducted with little fanfare by well-trained personnel elicits few objections. States do have the power to mandate sex education. Some legislatures require comprehensive family-life instruction; a few prohibit teaching birth control. However, the power to make most decisions about the specific content of the sex education curriculum rests largely with local school boards. This does not mean that a district can choose to have no content in the face of a state mandate. The Supreme Court of New Jersey, for example, upheld a regulation requiring a district to develop a family-life education program. But the program could include an "exclusal clause," meaning that parents who object to the curriculum can ask for an alternative assignment for their children.[6]

The state can require a course in sex education for all students. In a Maryland case the court dismissed the parents' free exercise argument and made no provision for the student to be excused on religious grounds.[7]

The courts also have ruled that the state — acting as *parens patria*, or parent of the country — has the right to determine health education for children. In a Connecticut case, a father claimed that it was his constitutional right to direct the upbringing and education of his son and demanded that the district excuse his child from health education because the curriculum contradicted some of his sincerely held beliefs. In particular, he claimed that parents have a constitutional right to challenge the school's AIDS awareness and sex education program. The court ruled that a parental challenge to a public school's AIDs awareness and sex education program was not rooted in a constitutionally protected right.[8]

A case in Maryland showed that required sex education as part of a school health curriculum does not violate First Amendment religious freedoms or the privacy rights of parents or children. The court ruled that these classes were an important public health measure that outweighs individual rights of privacy, parental control, or religious freedom.[9]

Openness in developing and delivering sexuality education often is the best way to steer clear of controversy. In 1982 the county school board under which I worked adopted human growth and development as a school subject for eighth-graders, and I was assigned to develop the local curriculum. Today, more than a decade later, that curriculum still is evolving and still being taught in our very conservative community. I attribute this fact to the community involvement that was built into the program. From the outset, my colleagues and I involved members of the community — physicians, business people, and ministers, as well as parents — in creating the curriculum. Furthermore, we introduced some safeguards:

- Only qualified personnel who feel comfortable with the subject are permitted to teach it.
- All materials are made available for parent review, and an outline of the course is sent home to parents at the beginning of the year.
- Instructors preview all materials so that there are no surprises.
- Questions of a personal nature are not asked — of either students or teachers.
- Factual reproductive information is presented in an objective manner.

These safeguards are valuable in avoiding problems, such as the incident that happened in one middle school — not part of our program — in which a teacher borrowed a film on reproduction but failed to preview it. As he was showing the film to his class, he became uncomfortable with the graphic presentation of a live birth and jumped in front of the screen, only to have the baby "born" on his white shirt. The event made the newspapers.

Evolution. In 1968 the Arkansas legislature passed an anti-evolution statute that was overturned in the U.S. Supreme Court. The Court found that the law was implicit state support of the Christian doctrine of creation and, in *Epperson* v. *Arkansas,* declared the law violated the First Amendment.[10] In 1981, the governor of Arkansas signed a bill that required balanced treatment of creationism and evolution in the public schools. Proponents maintained that not only was creationism a science, but that evolution was a kind of religion that they dubbed *secular humanism*. A federal court, in *McLean* v. *Arkansas Board of Education*, ruled that creationism was not a science but was imposing a belief that violated the First Amendment.[11]

In 1985 a federal district judge held that a Louisiana creation statute that was similar to the one in Arkansas was unconstitutional because "it promotes beliefs of some theistic sects to the detriment of others." This case, *Edwards* v. *Aguillar,* was appealed to the U.S. Supreme Court, where the statute was ruled unconstitutional.[12]

Legislatures in other states have continued to pass antievolution laws. The latest attempts are based on the theory of Intelligent Design, the idea that some phenomena are "irreducibly complex"; that is, they could not have occurred by the random accretion of traits but had to be the result of a design and designer. The designer, it is claimed, does not need to be God but had to be an intelligent force.

Several districts have jumped on the Intelligent Design bandwagon. In November 2005 the Kansas State Board of Education approved science standards that de-emphasized evolution and opened up a new media frenzy that some called the new Scopes trial. In November 2005, the state board of education of Kansas voted six to four to adopt revised academic standards that called for incorporating criticism of evolution in science courses. In Indiana, several state representatives sent letters to constituents arguing that Intelligent Design should get equal billing in science classes.

Perhaps the most famous case occurred in Dover, Pennsylvania, where the school district adopted the policy that Intelligent Design be taught in ninth-grade biology classes. Several parents, with ACLU support, filed a case in federal court claiming that intelligent design is an unconstitutional endorsement of religion. In November 2005, the eight members of the Dover school board who had backed the concept of Intelligent Design were voted out.

Afterward, the federal judge in charge of the case ruled that Intelligent Design was not science, but a religious idea that could not be taught in public school science classes.[13]

In January 2005, a federal judge in Georgia declared that a district's policy of requiring stickers that said that evolution is "a theory not a fact" be placed in science textbooks is an unconstitutional endorsement of religion. The district has appealed the ruling.[14] It seems clear that religious attacks against teaching evolution will continue.

Community Service. In recent years more and more school districts have begun to require students to perform community service as a graduation requirement. The state of Maryland has made such service a statewide requirement for graduation. Such "compulsory volunteerism," while contradictory in terminology, is an attempt on the part of schools (or governments) to instill a spirit of volunteerism in young people.

Benjamin Sendor, in an article for the *American School Board Journal* titled, "Service, Not Servitude," discusses how such a "compulsory volunteerism" policy played out in the Chapel Hill-Carrboro City School District. This district developed a requirement that students perform community service at a community agency to be chosen from a list provided by the district. The service was to be performed after school, on weekends, or during school holidays. Two students and their parents sued the school board, claiming that the policy violated the Thirteenth Amendment prohibition of involuntary servitude. Moreover, the policy violated due process rights and interfered with parents' right to control the upbringing of their children. However, the judge ruled that the provisions of the Thirteenth Amendment, written shortly after the Civil War, referred to slavery, not compulsory community service. Further, the required education program outweighed the parents' right to control the upbringing of their children in this case.[15]

In general the courts have decided that it is up to school boards to judge whether compulsory community service — "compulsory volunteerism" — is a sound way in which to instill community values in youth.

Animals in the Classroom. Here is a simple test. You are a second-grade teacher, and you believe it would be nice to have a pet in your classroom. Which of the following would be the best choice for a classroom pet?

a. a pine snake
b. a parrot
c. two white mice
d. a hamster

The best answer is: None of the above. The classroom is no place for pets. However, teachers may keep animals in the classroom in order to study animal behavior, to learn about their care, to observe how they live, or for other educational purposes. This is an important distinction.

In addition to the necessity of observing school and district regulations, teachers who desire to bring animals into the classroom — or to keep animals at school — must be aware of regulations affecting animal use that come from such community agencies as the public health service or the animal control department of local law enforcement. Activist groups, such as PETA (People for the Ethical Treatment of Animals), also may be involved in matters related to the educational use of animals. Animal abuse charges leveled at teachers, for example, can be serious matters; and conviction on such charges can carry stiff fines and other legal penalties — in addition to the loss of one's job.

School people may be held liable if an animal in the classroom bites a student, a staff member, or a visitor; if the animal passes a disease to a person; if a student has an allergic reaction to the animal's dander; and so on.

Science experiments that involve live animals also can create problems. It is wise to know the state and local laws regarding the use of live animals of any kind, including earthworms, for experimentation or dissection. In particular, experimentation involving live vertebrates is strictly controlled. Information can be obtained from state offices; for example, the Florida Game and Fresh Water Fish Commission, located in Tallahassee, publishes a leaflet titled, "Animals in the Classroom: What Are the Rules?"

Censorship

Censorship issues most often arise in schools when a parent challenges some aspect of the curriculum or a specific resource, such as a textbook, a library book, or a video. Some censorship challenges are broader and come from groups, rather than from a single parent or family.

A well-known case involved the Houghton Mifflin elementary reading series called *Impressions.* Some parents claimed that the series promoted belief in supernatural beings. The reading program, they said, "indoctrinates children in values, denies rights under both the First Amendment Establishment and Free Exercise Clause directly opposed to their Christian beliefs." The Seventh Circuit Court disagreed, finding that, while parents are free to provide their own religious instruction, the reading series did not cause children to either affirm or deny any religious doctrine. The court saw the teaching of reading and creativity, as well as tolerance for religious diversity, as appropriate for public schooling. The court asked the curriculum question: "What would become of elementary education. . . without such works as these. . . that expand the minds of young children and expand their sense of creativity."[16]

The question often arises over "selection" versus "censorship." School districts need to have clear, comprehensive policies in place regarding a multifaceted review of potential instructional materials prior to formal selection. The review process should include input from both school and community people, particularly parents. "Selection" is based on informed review, matching instructional materials to curricula. The issue of "censorship" — or attempts at censorship — arises when selected materials are challenged after they have been approved for use. Parents who have a legitimate objection to certain materials may ask that their children be given alternative reading assignments, for example. But when an individual or group tries to impose a narrow view on the whole school community and, therefore, to remove from use instructional materials that have been carefully selected, that constitutes censorship.

Few issues are more sensitive than those involving challenges to instructional materials on religious grounds. Indeed, the interplay of the Establishment Clause, the Religious Freedom Restoration Act, and the Free Speech Clause is confusing.

Religious Challenges and Rulings. The First Amendment provides: "Congress shall make no law respecting an establishment of religion." This Establishment Clause applies to all state government entities, including school districts and universities, through the Fourteenth Amendment. But note the tone of neutrality. While the state may not promote any particular religion, neither is it permitted to discriminate against religious beliefs.

Related to the issue of censorship is the issue of school prayer. Are schools "censoring" students' religious beliefs by prohibiting school prayer?

The form of school prayer in question is officially sanctioned group prayer. It has become a cliché to say that, as long as teachers give tests, students will pray. But individual — silent — prayer is not at issue. Group prayer and related activities are. In 1962 the U.S. Supreme Court decided that recitation of a school-composed prayer at the beginning of the school day violated the Establishment Clause.[17] In 1963 the Court also ruled that daily Bible reading and recitation of the Lord's Prayer also violated the neutral spirit of the Establishment Clause.[18]

In 1971 the Supreme Court heard a case — *Lemon* v. *Kurtzman* — that established a test of actions that violate the Establishment Clause.[19] This "Lemon Test," as it is called, includes the following:

- Does the action have a secular purpose?
- Is the primary effect of the action to advance or inhibit religion?
- Does the action foster excessive entanglement of government with religion?

One result of this test has been a cascade of other cases determining that prayer at school-sponsored events — such as graduation ceremonies, baccalaureate services, and sporting events — like prayer in the classroom, also is unconstitutional.

Some states have enacted statutes that permit (or promote) a "moment of silence" in lieu of a formal school prayer. However, such statutes do not provide a foot in the door to permit school prayer. Witness a 1985 decision that found that adding "voluntary prayer" to a required period of silence was unconstitutional.[20] *Lee* v. *Weisman*, decided in 1992, prohibits school employees from "coercing" students to participate in religious programs.[21]

The Religious Freedom Restoration Act was passed by Congress in 1993 with the purpose of restoring the law on free exercise of religion. The act requires government to justify burdening an individual's exercise of religion by showing 1) compelling government interest and 2) that it has used the least restrictive means of furthering that interest. Under the law, schools often decide to accommodate individuals by allowing them to opt out of aspects of the curriculum that may be repugnant to their beliefs.

In the fall of 1997 the Supreme Court declared the Religious Freedom Restoration Act unconstitutional. Some members of Congress are seeking to revive the act by changing provisions and debating it again. However, as of this writing, a state of indecision exists.

Several decisions have addressed censorship that seeks to limit access to materials that are objectionable to some people. Over the years, intolerance for the beliefs of others has subsided very little. Parents and others pose legal challenges to certain textbooks, films, courses, or programs and seek to have these materials removed from the curriculum. In *Board of Education* v. *Pico*, the Supreme Court reinforced that the school is a marketplace of ideas and never should become a place for the "pall of orthodoxy."[22] A current case involved books about Harry Potter, the broom-flying boy with the unruly hair and a lightning bolt imprinted on his forehead. The Cedarville, Arkansas, school board believed that he was a force of evil and ordered its libraries to put the book in a restricted area available only to those who had parental permission. In this case, *Counts* v. *Cedarville School District*, parents of Dakota Counts claimed that her First Amendment rights were violated, though they gave her permission to have access to any book in the library. Following the *Pico* rule, the court decided that restricting access to the book violated the constitution.[23] These cases reflect rulings for just the school library. Probably other cases involving the Harry Potter series will be forthcoming regarding its use in the classroom.

Other Objectionable Materials. Censorship attempts also occur on non-religious grounds. For example, Jane Doe, an African-American student in ninth-grade honors English, objected to two literary classics, Mark Twain's *Huckleberry Finn* and Faulkner's short story, *A Rose for Emily*, because of the repeated use of the word "nigger." Before the reading of the works, several black students in the school already had been targets of harassment, and the harassment appeared to increase after the assignment. The students complained to the school officials, who did nothing. Jane's mother filed suit in federal court claiming that her daughter's rights had been violated under the equal protection clause of the Fourteenth Amendment and Title VI of the Civil Rights Acts. She sought an injunction to stop using these books as required reading, but she did not object to their use as alternative readings. The lower court dismissed the suit, and she appealed to the Ninth Circuit. The case actually involved two issues: the content in the books and hateful slurs in the school environment that were not addressed.

The court sent the argument about the school's hostile environment back to the lower court to be addressed. But the court ruled that taking out materials would have a significant chilling effect on the board's right to establish curriculum and the student's right to read such books. They argued that such reasoning could lead to wide effects. For example, whites could seek to remove books by Maya Angelou and other black authors that portray whites in a negative manner. Jews might complain that Shakespeare was anti-Semitic, and so on. From this case, the message is clear: Teachers and students should not use the "N" word, but it is permissible in books.[24]

Copyright

An elementary teacher said, "I hate using this basal reader, but I have to. It's the law. So to get around it, I duplicate copies of an old anthology — to use the stories I want."

This teacher's confusion is interesting but not uncommon. States do not pass laws that require the use of a particular reader, though states may officially adopt certain materials for use in schools, and local school regulations may require that teachers teach from a given set of materials. But where the law does come into play is in duplicating the old anthology. That act, absent written permission from the copyright holder to do so, is a violation of copyright law.

As tempting as it is in times of tight budgets to copy expensive textbooks cheaply by using a handy office photocopier, educators need to think twice before violating copyright in this way. Modern technology has given users a ready way to become lawbreakers. To combat these abuses, in 1994 Congress passed the Copyright Act (P.L. 94-553). The growing use of computers prompted Congress to amend the act in 1998. The Digital Amendment to the Copyright Act protects material on the World Wide Web, including text, graphics, and even e-mail.

The purpose of copyright is to protect the rights of artists, authors, and so on, to derive income from their creative work. Using a copyrighted work "for educational purposes" does not excuse the user from the protections afforded to copyright holders by the law. Most books, periodicals, videotapes, computer programs, and other commercially produced educational materials are copyrighted. However, publications and other products of the U.S. government and state agencies are developed using taxpayer dollars and thus usually are not copyrighted.

It is impossible in the limited space of this brief guide to do more than touch on some basic principles, and educators should consult more detailed references about specific questions. However, a few general comments may be worthwhile.

Some use of copyrighted works without obtaining permission is acceptable under standards of "fair use." Fair use standards have varied over time and are affected by the amount of the work to be copied, the nature of the work, the purpose for which the work was created (commercial or noncommercial use), and the effect of the copying on the market value of the work. In some cases, educators can reproduce copyrighted material for non-profit, educational purposes if they plan to copy no more than 10% (or 1,000 words), if the motivation to copy is spontaneous and not at the direction of a supervisor, and if they use only a limited number of such copied works during a given course or school term.[25] See Figure 1 for some of the guidelines for fair use.

The law recognized the legitimate use of backup copies of computer programs in 1980, but such copies cannot be given away or sold. The making of multiple copies of computer programs, again absent specific permission, is a violation of copyright law. One form of "permission" in the case of computer programs may be a network license, which allows the sharing of a computer program among multiple users whose computers are connected, or "networked."

Videotapes also are subject to copyright restrictions, and taping programs from television broadcasts is an activity that carries a number of conditions. In some cases a television program may be spontaneously recorded and shown to a class; however, there are restrictions with regard to repeated showings. In no case can such "homemade" videotapes be kept for an extended period.

However, one popular teacher activity — photocopying consumable or workbook exercises, standardized tests, or answer sheets — is strictly illegal and does not constitute fair use.

Laws affecting the copying and use of all materials, but especially electronic resources, including cyberspace, are being developed as the Information Age unfolds. The rule of thumb to follow with respect to copying is, Ask. Many publishers and other instructional resource developers will gladly assist educators to use their works in as efficient and cost-effective a manner as possible.

Figure 1. Fair use guidelines for copyrighted materials.		
Brevity	**Spontaneity**	**Cumulative effect**
Poem or excerpts must not be over 250 words.	A teacher has an inspiration to use a work and no time to receive written permission.	Total number of works reproduced must not exceed nine instances per class per semester.
Stories, articles, essays of less than 250 words may be reproduced in complete form.	If the teacher wants to use the work the next semester, he must write for permission; he has ample time.	Only one complete piece and two excerpts from the same may be copied.
Excerpts of any prose work, such as a book or article, may be reproduced only up to 1,000 words or 10%, whichever is less.		Only three pieces from the same book or magazine.
Only one illustration, such as a photo, drawing, or diagram, may be reproduced from the same book or journal.		This limits the total number of articles, poems, excerpts that can be reproduced, even though brevity and spontaneity requirements may be met.
This criterion limits the length of material that can be reproduced and distributed from a single work.		

Notes

1. State v. Mizner, 50 Iowa 145 (Iowa 1878).
2. Mitchell v. McCall, 143 So. 2d 629 (Ala. 1962).
3. Tinker v. Des Moines Independent Community School District, 393 U.S. 503 (1969).
4. Mailloux v. Kiley, 448 F.2d 1242 (1st Cir. 1971).
5. Fowler v. Board of Education of Lincoln County, 819 F.2d 657 (6th Cir. 1987).
6. Smith v. Ricci, 446 A.2d 501 (N.J. 1982).
7. Cornwell v. State Bd. of Educ., 314 F. Supp. 340 (D. Md. 1969).
8. Leebaert v. Harrington, 332 F.3d 134 (2d Cir. 2003).
9. Cornwell v. Board, 314 F. Supp. 340 (D. Md. 1969); aff'd, 428 F.2d 471 (4th Cir. 1970). The Supreme Court declined to hear the case.
10. Epperson v. Arkansas, 393 U.S. 97 (1968).
11. McLean v. Arkansas Board of Education, 529 F. Supp. 1255 (E.D. Ark. 1982).
12. Edwards v. Aguillard, 482 U.S. 578 (1987).
13. Kitzmiller v. Dover Area School District, Case 4:04-cv-02688-JEJ, filed 12/20/2005.
14. Selman et al. v. Cobb County School District, No. 1 02-cv-2325-CC (N.D. Ga. January 13, 2005)
15. Benjamin Sendor, "Service, Not Servitude," *American School Board Journal* 183 (May 1996): 5, 16, 39.
16. Fleischfresser v. Directors of Sch. Dist. 200, 15 F.3d 680 (7th Cir. 1994).
17. Engel v. Vitale, 370 U.S. 421 (1962).
18. School District of Abington Township v. Schempp, 374 U.S. 203 (1963).
19. Lemon v. Kurtzman, 403 U.S. 602 (1971).
20. Wallace v. Jaffree, 472 U.S. 38 (1985).
21. Lee v. Weisman, 505 U.S. 577 (1992).
22. Board of Education v. Pico, 457 U.S. 853 (1982).
23. Counts v. Cedarville School District, 295 F. Supp. 2d 996 (W.D. Ark.. 2003).
24. Monteiro v. Tempe Union High School District, 158 F.3d 1022 (9th Cir. 1998).
25. Kenneth T. Murray, "Copyright and the Educator," *Phi Delta Kappan* 75 (March 1994): 552-55.

Chapter Six

SUPERVISION AND DISCIPLINE

You are an elementary principal. Your school advisory council has developed a tough "zero tolerance" policy regarding any type of weapon. A student who brings a weapon to school — with or without malicious intent — is to be given an immediate one-day suspension. A kindergarten teacher reports that one of her students has a metal fingernail file and is waving it around. Is the fingernail file a weapon? What do you do?

A Florida elementary principal had to make this decision. Following the principle that "zero tolerance is zero tolerance," he suspended the five-year-old for one day. Of course, the action made headlines in the local and national newspapers.

Such are the dilemmas in supervision. Can a rule be bent? Should it be bent, using judgment and discretion? In this case, was the principal right to stick to the "zero tolerance" rule? Should the teacher have ignored the incident or simply told the student to put away the nail file? What if the student later took out the file during recess and injured another student? Should the teacher have confiscated the file and then had a conference with the student's parents?

Many school districts are faced with similar questions when absolute rules — such as zero tolerance for weapons, drugs, or other substances — meet the realities of day-to-day supervision of children and adolescents.

Reason and Supervision

The law requires educators to provide adequate supervision of students and vests much of that responsibility in those who work most directly with students, teachers and principals. However, supervision of students must be tempered by reason.

(Incidentally, the same holds true for the relationship between teachers and administrators. The principal — and, ultimately, the school board — is responsible for the supervision of teachers. He or she may assign certain responsibilities, ranging from what classes to teach to which halls to monitor, to teachers; but those assignments must be reasonable.)

Therefore educators must exercise reasonable care to protect students from hazards, in particular while students are on school property but, in many cases, also as students travel to and from school and when they are involved in school-related activities and programs outside the regular instructional day. Schools and individual educators can be held liable if harm occurs when supervision is absent or negligently performed.

For example, in an extended-day program in a Florida district, a fourth-grade student, who was not enrolled in the program, joined the group for viewing a solar eclipse. The group was instructed in the proper way of looking at the eclipse, but the guest student looked directly at the sun and suffered permanent eye damage. Did the teacher of the extended-day program have a duty of care for the guest student?

While a lower court ruled for the teacher in this case, the appeals court ruled that the matter involved the issue of reasonable supervision. Because the teacher permitted the student guest to join the group, she also accepted the duty of care to provide supervision that would keep the student from harm. Thus the appeals court reversed the lower court's decision and ordered a new trial.[1]

Many cases have been brought before the courts over the injury of a student while the teacher was absent from the classroom. In most cases the central question is: Did the teacher's absence contribute directly to the injury? In addition to questions about the teacher's reason for being absent and the length of the absence, the courts consider — as teachers must in making the decision to leave the classroom — the age and maturity of the students, the students' general mental capacity (knowledge of right and wrong behavior, for example), and the nature of the classroom activity at the time of the absence.

The test in court is the same test that educators must apply to themselves: What would a reasonable and prudent person do under the circumstances?

Most principals tell their teachers never to leave students alone in a classroom (or gym, auditorium, playing field, and so on). But emergencies can arise. When they do, reasonable supervision standards require the teacher who must leave the classroom to notify the office or a colleague so that supervision can be provided in some alternative manner. (For related matters involving negligence, see Chapter Three.)

Supervision of Students with Disabilities

During the 1980s more than 60% of legal cases involving education issues focused on matters involving students with disabilities. Cases involving students with disabilities are treated somewhat differently because, depending on the issue, they may be governed by federal law, rather than state law.

To tackle issues of supervision related to handicapped students, one must recognize three laws. In 1973 the Vocational Rehabilitation Act (often referred to in education circles by the pertinent part, Section 504) introduced regulations for addressing the needs of handicapped children. It is applicable to all agencies receiving federal funds. This act affects local districts and the way they must educate students with disabilities. States have the obligation to provide all children with a "free and appropriate" education (FAPE) under the Rehabilitation Act of 1973, Section 504. In 1982 an appellate court ruled that New Mexico, a state that did not participate in federal funding, still was obligated under Section 504.[2]

The second major piece of legislation came in 1975. Titled the Education of All Handicapped Children Act, it has become better known simply as Public Law 94-142. Recently this legislation has been revisited in the third major law, the 1990 Individuals with Disabilities Education Act (IDEA), which incorporates much of the earlier legislation, as well as the results from litigation during the 1970s and 1980s. This law is designed to ensure handicapped children's rights to appropriate education.

Legal rulings on issues related to the education of students with disabilities are guided by IDEA in several ways:

- IDEA focuses on the individual, and each student is required to have an Individual Educational Plan (IEP) developed cooperatively by the student's parents, teachers, and education specialists.
- Parents are empowered under IDEA to be individually involved in the specifics of their child's education; parent involvement in regular education is more general, and regular education is less individualized.
- Under IDEA, legal accountability for education is governed by a comprehensive set of procedural guidelines.
- Because IDEA is a federal law, its application is overseen by federal agencies, including the Department of Education and the Office of Civil Rights; regular education is a state responsibility, and much of that responsibility is delegated to local school boards.

Chapter 9 addresses special education law in depth.

School-Related Activity Cases

Of all school-related activities, few are as potentially problematic as field trips. Taking students out of the relatively controlled setting of the school can present a number of supervision challenges.

Field trips are exciting. After all, one reason to take students on field trips is to stimulate thought, learning, and imagination. But teachers also can get caught up in the excitement, sometimes to the point of neglecting their duty of care. A teacher and six other adult chaperones took 35 preschool and elementary children to the beach. Four children posed on a large log for the teacher to take pictures. The teacher had her back to the ocean and did not see a large wave about to surge to the shore. The wave lifted the log and the children fell off; one child was crushed under the log. The court concluded that the possibility of the wave coming ashore was common knowledge in the ocean area, and the teacher had breached her duty to supervise.[3]

On the other hand, students also can be expected to exercise judgment in keeping with their maturity. A 13-year-old boy was hit by a car while crossing the street during a field trip. The court found that the student did not have vision or hearing problems and understood the safety precautions necessary to safely cross a street. Although the teacher had given the student permission to cross the street, it was the student's responsibility to do so safely. The court found that the teacher was not negligent in supervisory duties.[4]

Even with reasonable supervision, the unanticipated can happen. A nine-year-old boy was killed during a lunch recess when he was accidentally struck by a bat swung by another student. At the time of the accident, the supervising teacher was 45 feet away helping a kindergarten student. The court found that the teacher was exercising reasonable supervision; the accident was not foreseeable.[5]

Overnight trips present special challenges. Despite risks and strict liability under these conditions, most districts give staff little guidance about overnight trips. Ronald Hyman, a New Jersey law professor writing in the *School Superintendent's Insider*,[6] makes some suggestions that districts and schools should consider for overnight trips:

- Have a meeting of chaperones and students to read the district policy and student code of conduct on field trips. Make sure adequate chaperones are available. Take a copy of the code of conduct with you.
- Remind students that all district rules apply during class trips. Review each of these rules.

- Students must respect each other. This means no bullying, harassment, fighting, hazing, or other misconduct.
- Students must report any misconduct.
- Staff and chaperones must be vigilant about enforcing school rules on the trip, and students can expect serious disciplinary action, such as suspension or expulsion for misconduct.
- Students' property can be subjected to searches.
- Be constantly vigilant. Staff must supervise, including middle of the night inspections, and never let older students go out on their own during a field trip.
- Conduct reasonable searches. The district can require parents of all students in overnight trips to consent to a search of their children's hand luggage before boarding the bus.
- Send a memo home that gives all the above expectations, including the search of any personal property when there is reasonable suspicion that students are violating school rules or the law. These searches can occur any time, including while students are in hotel rooms or before boarding the bus. Several court decisions have upheld the right to search students' possessions or hotel rooms during field trips.
- Don't send students home alone. If someone has broken the rules, call the parents and release him or her only to the parents. If it involves drugs or weapons, call law enforcement. In a New York case, a student committed suicide after his teacher discovered drugs, called the police, and sent him home alone.

In Search of "Reasonableness"

The right — and obligation — to control the behavior of students in school has been established under the common law doctrine called *in loco parentis*. The Latin phrase means "in place of the parent." A Nebraska court defined the doctrine, stating that "general education and control of pupils who attend public school are in the hands of principals and teachers. This control extends to health, proper surroundings, necessary discipline, promotion of morality, and other wholesome influences, while parental authority is temporarily suspended."[7]

The doctrine of *in loco parentis* is incorporated into a number of states' laws; but even in states where the doctrine has not been formalized, it has been held as common law. This is not to say that variations in interpretation do not occur. In fact, the doctrine fell out of favor in the 1960s only to resurge strongly in the 1970s. But the doctrine offers a double-edged sword. For example, schools can employ corporal punishment (where it is not prohibited by law), but they still are expected to maintain a standard of care equivalent to a conscientious parent, a parent who might not approve of corporal punishment.

Unlike parents, who cannot entirely shed their parental responsibilities, schools can remove students from the education setting under certain conditions. This power to suspend a student from school, at least for a short period, normally is delegated by the school board to the principal; the principal cannot, in turn, delegate this power to the teacher — in most cases. In 1996 a Florida law was enacted that does give teachers the authority to remove disruptive students from class and to request alternative placement for them. This measure was seen as a reasonable way to assist teachers in fulfilling their responsibility for maintaining order and discipline in order to be able to teach.

"Reasonableness" is broadly construed to apply to regulations that maintain and advance the educational process. School and classroom rules cannot be so broad or vague as to allow for arbitrary or capricious application. But neither is it advisable to make rules so narrow and tight that a reasonable exception cannot be made — as in the case of the nail file as a weapon. Moreover, an important factor in judging the reasonableness of a rule (or set of rules) is the extent to which students and parents are clearly informed about the expected behaviors. The in loco parentis right, as interpreted by the courts, is bound by two standards: reasonableness and good faith without malice. These standards bear remembering, particularly with regard to disciplinary actions directed at students.

Notions of reasonableness also affect interpretations of students' rights in other areas, including the expression of their beliefs or convictions.

Saluting the Flag. A New York court held that a school could not require a student to stand for the Pledge of Allegiance, nor could it ask a student who did not stand to leave the classroom. Symbolic protest — choosing not to stand — is protected expression to which students have a right, provided that the protest does not disturb or disrupt the educational process.[8]

Demonstrating for a Cause. Students may assemble peaceably to demonstrate for a cause; however, schools can impose restrictions with regard to time, place, or manner of demonstration if such restrictions ensure that the educational process will not be disrupted by the protest.

Student Dress

Perhaps no area of supervision and discipline has been as volatile as student dress, particularly apparel that is seen as free expression. For the past quarter-century, many cases involving issues of student dress as expression have harkened to the High Court's decision in a case called *Tinker v. Des Moines Independent Community School District.*

In 1969 the U.S. Supreme Court issued the landmark *Tinker* decision, which declared that "students in school as well as out of school are 'persons' under our Constitution."[9] In this case the school board of Des Moines, Iowa, refused to let a group of students protest the Vietnam War by wearing black armbands. The Court ruled that the school board's action was unconstitutional and that the rights of students may not be regulated unless school authorities can show a material and substantial disruption of school work and discipline.

The oft-heard phrase is that students do not shed their constitutional rights at the schoolhouse door. School boards must be able to justify — usually on educational grounds — limitation or curtailment of freedoms. Of course, students cannot disrupt classes or invade the rights of others; but such "limitations" are little different from the "limitation" to free speech that does not allow a noisy person to disturb the peace of his neighbor. The courts balance concerns for individual freedom with the need for an orderly environment, an environment in the case of schools that is conducive to learning.

The *Tinker* case notwithstanding, some expressions can be viewed as disruptive. For example, in a Tennessee case the court held that a rule against wearing "provocative symbols," though broad and vague, was sufficient to let stand the suspension of a student for wearing a Confederate flag patch. The symbol had been banned because it was seen as the cause of racial disturbances at the school in the previous year.[10]

The more general matter of student dress can be taken up apart from dress as symbolic expression of a particular political or social belief. Schools often have sought to control what students wear for various reasons, such as equating orderly dress to orderly learning, avoiding class distinctions through the use of standardized dress or uniforms, and so on. During the 1960s and 1970s the issue of school dress (and grooming) gave rise to more litigation than almost any other issue except desegregation. But decisions fell in all directions, which further complicated matters. However, no case involving student dress or grooming has ever been accepted by the U.S. Supreme Court.

In April 1972 the U.S. 5th Circuit Court of Appeals ruled that the right to wear one's hair as desired is not protected by the U.S. Constitution. The court also rejected arguments that dress codes violate rights protected under the First, Eighth, Ninth, Tenth, and Fourteenth Amendments.[11]

Students' T-shirts or other pieces of apparel that carry displays or statements that are sexually or otherwise offensive to the public may be prohibited. A Massachusetts court ruled that "inappropriate language" on T-shirts (some statements were offensive and demeaning to women) interfered with the school's mission and, therefore, could be banned by school officials.[12]

Standardized-dress proposals, including the requirement that students wear uniforms, have received a good deal of attention, particularly in recent years. But the issue is larger than individuality versus conformity, which often is how it is characterized. The real question is whether uniforms serve to improve education, in part by eliminating the distractions of different — often differentiating — dress. Some prominent educators have made the case for requiring school uniforms.[13] One reason is that uniforms may blunt visible class distinctions.

The guiding principle in dealing with student dress goes back to notions about reasonableness. Schools can restrict — in some cases, dictate — student dress, as long as the restrictions are neither unreasonable nor arbitrary. Restrictions are permitted that are intended to accomplish a legitimate objective related to the educational mission of the schools. When such restrictions are taken to court, the burden usually is on the challenger to show that the restrictions are unwarranted.

More recently, concerns about student dress have focused on dress as an expression of gang affiliation. For many gangs, certain articles of clothing, how clothes are worn, and the symbols displayed on one's clothes are marks of distinction. Dress serves to communicate affiliation. More than a decade ago, the *Chicago Tribune* (4 April 1995, p. 181) carried a story about a student innocently wearing a gold, six-pointed star, the traditional symbol of his Jewish faith. However, law enforcement officers in Harvard, Illinois, also knew that the symbol sometimes was associated with street gangs. When the student left school, the police arrested him and charged him with violating an ordinance aimed at cracking down on gangs.

In another Illinois case a high school student was suspended under a school dress code prohibiting the wearing of gang symbols. The student wore an earring that marked gang membership. The student sued, claiming that the dress code was a violation of his free-speech rights. However, the court upheld the dress code, saying that wearing the earring denoted gang membership and the restriction was intended to prevent gang violence in school.[14]

Using dress to identify with groups other than gangs also may be restricted if other concerns are overriding. For example, schools prohibit certain forms of dress because they present hazards: ties and necklaces (which can get tangled in machinery), sagging trousers or floor-length skirts (which can trip students on stairs), and so on. In a case in New Mexico, a student claimed that the school dress code prohibiting saggy pants violated his rights. He contended the style, known as "hip hop," had African-American roots and wearing that style of pants was a matter of group identity. The court held to the contrary because the practice of "sagging" (wearing saggy pants) was not speech or expressive conduct protected by the First Amendment.[15]

On the other hand, schools must have a good reason to ban dress that identifies with a group. A California court ruled that a school dress code that prohibited identifying with professional or college sports teams violated the free speech rights of elementary and middle school students but not high school students. The court made a distinction that the schools had chosen to overlook: There was negligible gang activity in middle and elementary schools; therefore the wearing of identifying clothing posed no threat of disruption. However, at the high school, where the wearing of team-related apparel was a gang marker, the school could justifiably prohibit such clothing.[16]

Discipline and Punishment

Schools must prevent violence. One aspect of prevention may be to prohibit the wearing of gang-identification apparel, as noted in the previous section. So-called zero-tolerance measures — recall the illustration that opened this chapter — also are aimed at ensuring an orderly environment, one that is free of weapons, drugs, and so on.

Some schools have begun to use metal detectors to prevent violence by making it more difficult to bring weapons into the school. A New York state court held that the use of a hand-held metal detector was acceptable in a high school known for high crime on the ground that security interests outweighed privacy interests.[17]

The Gun-Free Schools Act (20 U.S.C. Section 8921), passed in 1994, compels all states receiving federal funds to enact laws requiring school officials to expel for one year any student who brings a gun to school. However, the law allows school officials to modify the punishment on a case-by-case basis. At the same time, states also are permitted to toughen the new law by expanding their statutes to include more than guns. For example, Ohio allows expulsion of students who bring knives to school.

To bring the IDEA in line with the Gun-Free Schools Act, Congress passed the Jeffords Amendment, which provides that a student with a disability who brings a firearm to school may be removed to an alternative placement for up to 45 days while the other IDEA procedures for changing a placement are followed.

Types of Discipline

Discipline may vary from school district to school district, depending on the nature of the infraction, the disciplinary record of the student, and other circumstances. Discipline measures span the continuum from a simple verbal warning to permanent expulsion from the district's schools.

Grade Reduction and Academic Sanctions. Courts usually defer to schools in matters of policy on academic decisions unless the policy is arbitrary, malicious, or capricious. Students and parents who contend that a grade was given unfairly have brought cases seeking a change in the grade; but courts routinely deny these requests unless it can be shown that the teacher was arbitrary, capricious, or malicious. Schools should not drop grades because students engaged in prohibited behaviors, such as smoking or events not occurring at school. In a 1993 case, a federal court held that a high school's rule to reduce grades 4% for each day of suspension for alcohol-related misconduct violated substantive due process.[18]

A student's grades may be reduced because of absences or frequent tardies. Courts have upheld grade reduction for being absent or truant on the theory that grades should reflect effort, including class attendance and performance.[19]

Withholding Diplomas. Here the rule is similar to grading: Academic rewards should reflect academic accomplishment. If the student has earned a diploma — even though he or she has engaged in misconduct — the diploma should not be withheld. If the student has not fulfilled the requirements for the diploma, the district is under no obligation to issue one.

Exclusions from Extracurricular Activities. In numerous cases students have sued because of removal from extracurricular activities for discipline. The courts have been very consistent in holding that due process protections do not apply because no liberty or property interests are involved. In a 1992 Arkansas case, the court cited rulings in numerous cases that found expelling or suspending students from extracurricular activities does not violate their due process rights.[20] Concerning athletic suspensions, state rules or state athletic association rules may dictate procedures that a school must follow before imposing an athletic suspension.

Corporal Punishment. While many schools and educators view corporal punishment as counterproductive to efforts to reduce violence, others see the use of such punishment as reasonable and necessary to the maintenance of an orderly educational environment. The courts have been somewhat divided on this matter — as have state legislatures. However, common law lays stress on certain conditions with regard to corporal punishment. Such punishment must be neither unreasonable nor excessive. Consideration must be given to the nature of the offense, the maturity and sex of the offender, and the severity of the punishment to be inflicted. The punishment must be delivered without anger or malice.

Schools and educators that employ corporal punishment can expose themselves to charges of assault and battery if the student (or the student's parents) brings suit. The courts will examine the matters noted in the previous paragraph, but they also will look at the question of reasonableness from the standpoint of the rule being enforced. Was the rule itself reasonable, and was corporal punishment a reasonable response to violation of the rule?

In some locations corporal punishment has been banned, but such a ban is not universal in spite of the efforts of some groups to make it so. In the past, foes of corporal punishment often claimed that it is "cruel and unusual" and thus violated the Eighth Amendment. In 1977, however, the U.S. Supreme Court decided that the "cruel and unusual" punishment standard applied to criminal offenses, not school offenses. In the Dade County, Florida, case the Court also ruled that no formal due process procedure was required prior to the administration of corporal punishment.[21]

As a result of this case, the use of corporal punishment can be sanctioned. When permitted by law and school board policy and when administered in a reasonable manner, corporal punishment does not violate students' rights. No due process is required, and punishment may be administered against the wishes of the parents (though most principals are hesitant to do this). However, "when permitted by law" is a key phrase. In jurisdictions where corporal punishment is not permitted, either by state law or school regulations, school employees may be liable for battery charges if they use corporal punishment of any kind. In a New York case involving a bus monitor who slapped a misbehaving student, the court held that any person who hits a child for any reason other than self-defense is liable for money damages for the tort of battery.[22]

Self-Defense. Some violence is directed by students at other students, but some students also direct violent acts toward teachers and administrators. In such cases self-defense may become an issue. Most states recognize the legitimacy of using force in self-defense. A few states — Florida, for example — make it a third-degree felony to commit assault or battery on a school employee.

In protecting oneself through the use of force, the test of whether such force was necessary will be that force was used to prevent death or serious injury.

Related to this issue is the question of who is responsible when a student assaults or batters a teacher. While students may be punished for their violent acts, in many cases the parents of students also can be held liable. For example, the parents of a student diagnosed with attention deficit hyperactivity disorder decided not to give the boy a drug that reduced the student's aggressive behavior. Later the student assaulted a teacher by pulling her to the floor by the hair and injuring her neck. The teacher won the judgment against the parents, who were found negligent for not informing school personnel of their decision to discontinue the medicine.[23]

Suspension. While a few discipline and punishment issues can be resolved without reference to due process, most cases require adherence to the Fourteenth Amendment standard of not depriving "any person of life, liberty, or property without due process of law." Denial of the right of due process often equates to presuming a person guilty, which violates a major premise of our judicial system.[24]

Four elements of justice must be present for due process: adequate notice of charges, reasonable opportunity to prepare a defense against those charges, an orderly hearing consistent with the case, and a fair and impartial decision.

Whether the suspension is in school or out-of-school, the U.S. Supreme Court in the landmark case, *Goss* v. *Lopez*, has ruled that exclusion from educational services requires some form of due process.[25] For an out-of-school suspension of less than 10 days, the hearing may be more spontaneous and informal with these minimal requirements:

- Oral or written notice of the charges.
- An opportunity to explain, deny, or admit the charges or evidence.
- Decision must be based on the evidence heard.

While guidelines for suspensions of less than 10 days usually are not spelled out, suspensions over 10 days have more specific guidelines. Expulsion requires a full hearing before the board, and the following items must be observed:

- Written note of specific charges.
- Sufficient time between the notice and hearing to allow the student to prepare a defense.
- Right to present evidence and examine witnesses and the right to counsel.
- The decision must made on the merits of the case by an impartial panel.

The Court did note that the degree of formality in due process proceedings could vary with the severity of the penalty. The Court also ruled that no delay between the time of notice and time of hearing is required. The disciplinarian must explain his or her version of the facts, and there must be at least an informal give and take. The Court did not impose a requirement of trial-like proceedings or witnesses because it realized that such a requirement could be overwhelming.

Expulsion of a student is an extension of suspension, in that the student is prohibited from attending school for a longer period of time. Permanent expulsion is rare, but in many districts a student may be expelled for the remainder of a semester or school year. Expulsion requires formal application of due process standards.

Suspension is a particularly sticky issue when it is considered as punishment for a student's behavior that may be related to a disability. In general the courts have agreed that students with disabilities may not be expelled and may be suspended only under extreme circumstances, usually for a period of time to allow for application of IDEA placement procedures (as noted previously). Behavior is regarded as related to a disability only if the disability impairs the student's behavioral controls. For example, a physical disability probably is not behaviorally related.[26]

When a disability is not behaviorally related, school authorities may use the same suspension standards that apply to other students. However, if a student is to be suspended for more than 10 days, then the school must change the student's placement using the IDEA procedures.

Writing Disciplinary Referrals

Because many suspensions are based on teacher discipline referrals, the teacher must know how to write a quality referral. Woodrow Clymer, director of Employee Relations in the Marion County, Florida, District Schools, encourages his deans and assistant principals to teach teachers to write a referral that cannot be misunderstood.[27] Here are some of the pointers that he lists:

- When writing the referral, be specific. Describe what happened. For example, if a student cursed the teacher, do not just write "disrespectful." Write exactly what the student said.
- If the offense is continued classroom misconduct, be sure to document the previous things the student has done and what interventions you have used, for example, warning, moving the student's seat, notes to parent, calling a parent. A referral should not be given unless your have tried basic management strategies.
- If the student was fighting, be sure to describe this carefully. In many states this can lead to interventions by law enforcement.
- Do not mention the names of other students on the referral. If you are giving two students a referral, do not include the names, and be sure to write a separate referral for each student.
- Do not write in red or use exclamation marks. For example, "I will not tolerate this behavior!!!!!!!!!!!!" Exclamation marks are like shouting at the person in charge of discipline as well as at the parent.
- Do not write the referral in anger or be unprofessional in any way. Never include comments like, "He is acting like a fool" or "He should be back in kindergarten."

- Read the referral over, not to be just understood, but so that you will never be misunderstood.
- Remember, several people will be reading this referral: the student, the person in charge of discipline, parents, and perhaps district personnel.
- When the student returns to school, try to help him or her understand that, though you do not condone the behavior, you are there to help the student be successful in school. Do not be vindictive.

Notes

1. Vesprill v. School Bd. of Orange County, 641 So. 2d 883 (Fla. Dist. Ct. App. 1994).
2. New Mexico Ass'n for Retarded Citizens v. New Mexico, 678 E.2d 847 (10th Cir. 1982).
3. Morris v. Douglas Co. Sch. Dist., 403 P.2d 775 (Oreg. 1965).
4. King v. Kastanson, 720 S.W.2d 6 (Tenn. App. 1986).
5. Ferguson v. Desoto Parish School Bd., 467 So. 2d 1257 (La. App. 1985).
6. Ronald Hyman, "Overnight Trips," *School Superintendent's Insider* (April 2005): 7.
7. Richardson v. Brahan, 249 N.W. 557 (Neb. 1933).
8. Goetz v. Ansell, 477 F.2d 636 (2d Cir. 1973).
9. Tinker v. Des Moines Independent Community School District, 393 U.S. 503 (1969).
10. Melton v. Young, 328 F. Supp. 88 (E.D. Tenn. 1971).
11. *See, e.g.*, Karr v. Schmidt, 460 F.2d 609 (5th Cir. 1972).
12. Pyle v. South Hadley School Comm., 861 F. Supp. 157 (D. Mass. 1994), *vacated, question certified*, 55 F.3d 20 (1st Cir. 1996).
13. Peter Caruso, "Individuality vs. Conformity: The Issues Behind School Uniforms," *NASSP Bulletin* (September 1996): 83-88.
14. Olesen v. Bd. of Education, 676 F. Supp. 820 (N.D. Ill. 1987).
15. Green v. Albuquerque Pub. School., 899 F. Supp. 556 (D. N.M. 1995).
16. Jeglin v. San Jacinto Unified Sch. Dist., 827 F. Supp. 1459 (C.D. Calif. 1993).
17. People v. Dukes, 580 N.Y.S.2d 850 (N.Y. Crim. Ct. 1992).
18. Smith v. School District of Hobart, 811 F. Supp. 391 (N.D. Ind. 1993).
19. Williams v. Board of Education of Marranna School District, 626 S.W.2d 361 (Ark. 1982).
20. McFarlin v. Newport Special School District, 784 F. Supp. 589 (E.D. Ark. 1992).
21. Ingraham v. Wright, 430 U.S. 651 (1977).

22. Rodriguez v. Johnson, 504 N.Y.S.2d 379 (N.Y. 1986).
23. Nieuwendorp v. American Family Insur. Co., 529 N.W.2d 594 (Wis. 1995).
24. Bruce Meredith and Julie Underwood, "Irreconcilable Differences? Defining the Rising Conflict Between Regular and Special Education," *Journal of Law and Education* 24 (Spring 1995): 195-235.
25. Goss v. Lopez, 419 U.S. 565 (1975).
26. Doe v. Maher, 793 F.2d 1470 (9th Cir. 1986); *aff'd in part, modified in part*, Honig v. Doe, 484 U.S. 305 (1988).
27. Interview with Woodrow Clymer, director of Employee Relations, Marion County, Florida, District Schools, 28 October 2005.

Chapter Seven

PROPERTY AND PRIVACY

Y ou are the vice principal of an intermediate school. At 9:10 in the morning you notice that two of your students, both carrying their purses, are wandering off campus to a place where students have been known to smoke marijuana. You and a security guard go to the area and smell marijuana. Do you have a "reasonable cause" for searching the girls' purses?

Administrators in such situations must make several quick decisions. To search or not to search is one decision. What are the reasons for the search? The principal must mentally list the reasons for the search so that those reasons later can be documented in writing. In this case, which was decided by a court in 1989, the girl who sued claimed that no one saw her smoking and, therefore, the search was unreasonable — even though the principal and the security guard did find marijuana in her purse. The principal won this case because his reasons were valid and he was able to readily defend his actions.[1]

When students bring illegal items to school — drugs or guns, for example — then school officials have an obligation to respond, usually by confiscating the illegal items and involving law enforcement authorities. But teachers sometimes are tempted to confiscate and destroy items that are merely bothersome, such as water pistols and comic books. Yielding to that temptation can create problems.

Schools may make rules that forbid students to bring certain items into the school setting, if the items are deemed to interfere with the educational process. However, they also need to develop procedures for confiscation and later return of most items. For example, a water pistol might be confiscated if it is seen in a student's possession and then returned to the student at the close of the school day or the end of the semester. Or, for certain confiscated items, the school might return them only to the student's parent.

Absent reasonable rules, educators run the risk of being accused of "trespass of private personal property," or intentionally taking or interfering with the use of another's possessions without authority to do so. This intentional tort is one of the most common torts committed by teachers.

Searches and "Reasonable Cause"

The Fourth Amendment contains a "probable cause" standard that often is invoked when the school's authority is challenged, usually as a result of searching students' persons or property, such as vehicles or school lockers. While the Fourth Amendment does not necessarily govern search and seizure in the schools, school officials must exercise good judgment in their search and seizure policies and practices.

Personal Searches. A standard test for searches of individuals (including clothing and immediate possessions, such as purses or book bags) was adopted by the U.S. Supreme Court in a 1985 case in New Jersey.[2] In that case a teacher reported that a girl was smoking in the restroom. The girl denied it, but a search of her purse revealed cigarettes, marijuana, and drug paraphernalia. When the case reached the High Court, school officials were found not to be constrained by "probable cause" under the Fourth Amendment but to operate under the common law doctrine of *in loco parentis.* Thus school officials are allowed to conduct a search of a student's purse if they have a reasonable suspicion that the search will produce evidence of an illegal possession. This standard also was applied in the 1989 case described at the beginning of this chapter.

This is not to say that the Fourth Amendment does not apply in a school setting. Rather, it applies generally but with a less stringent test than that which is applied to searches by law enforcement officials. Police searches are governed by the Fourth Amendment's "probable cause" standard, while a search by school officials is governed by a lesser, "reasonable cause" standard. The search must be reasonable in light of the age and experience of the student and the nature of the infraction. There also must be reasonable grounds for the search — in other words, some concrete evidence, not merely general suspicion — and the scope of the search must be focused, rather than general or random.

Strip Searches. School officials must exercise extreme caution in conducting any form of so-called strip search, which would require the student to remove his or her clothing. This type of personal search is highly intrusive and likely to be considered unreasonable in the courts. For example, in 1977, a New York school official conducted a strip search of an entire fifth-grade class because three dollars were missing. A federal court ruled that this strip search was unreasonable and unconstitutional.[3] While the courts have permitted such searches in extreme cases,[4] searches for evidence that may result in criminal charges and that require students to disrobe should be conducted by law enforcement officials, who are held to the full probable-cause and warrant requirements of the Fourth Amendment.

Locker and Desk Searches. Two students reported that a third student had a gun and intended to retaliate for a previous altercation. School officials searched that student's locker and found a rifle. When the case went to trial, the court held that the search did not violate the Fourth Amendment because an immediate response from school personnel was needed; therefore the expectation of privacy asserted by the student was unreasonable.[5]

School officials, by creating an appropriate policy, also may inspect students' desks and lockers on a regular, publicized basis.

Students are not entitled to the expectation of privacy in desks and lockers, because school officials have master keys.[6] Nor do school officials have any obligation to warn students about their rights before such searches.[7]

Automobile Searches. Students' vehicles, while on school property, also may be subject to search under the "reasonable cause" standard. For example, based on a tip that a student was selling drugs in the school parking lot, administrators searched the student and found a large amount of money and a list of telephone numbers. In later searching the student's car, they found a briefcase containing marijuana. When the school officials' actions were later challenged, the court ruled that the personal search was reasonable; and the subsequent search of the students' automobile was warranted because the automobile could have been removed.[8]

Dog Sniff Searches. The use of dogs to sniff for drugs or firearms without entering lockers or cars is not considered to be a "search" in the formal sense; therefore the action is not bound to the "reasonable cause" standard. When a dog alerts officials, however, a more intrusive search may be warranted, which would be in line with the "reasonable cause" standard.[9]

On the other hand, using dogs to sniff a student as a means of drug detection is considered to be a search and will likely be considered as unreasonable unless the action is based on an individualized suspicion that is supported by specific information. Using dogs to sniff groups of students or individual students at random is generally considered to be unreasonable.

Privacy at Issue

Searches invade students' privacy, and so they must be made only according to the "reasonable cause" standard. But what about other invasions of privacy? Schools often believe they have a reasonable cause — often in the name of keeping students safe by preventing drug abuse, violence, or other crimes — for invading students' privacy, either persons or property. Drug testing is an example.

Some schools use drug testing. However, they usually are seen as violating students' privacy rights when they require all students to submit to blood or urine tests. An Arkansas Court, for example, ruled that there were less obtrusive (and intrusive) ways to determine rule infraction.[10]

A New Jersey school board required students to have annual exams that included a urinalysis. If a student tested positive for drugs, then district officials notified the student's parents, hoping that the parents would then get treatment for the student. The court ruled that this procedure was unreasonable.[11]

While general drug testing has been seen as unreasonable, specific drug testing has been allowed — for example, when it is limited to extracurricular athletics.

For example, the *Vernonia* case involved a student who objected to a routine drug test that was required for participation in the school's sports program. In that case, the court ruled that students who are in athletics and other highly visible extracurricular activities have a diminished expectation of privacy. The court ruled that schools may carry out certain suspicionless searches, such as random drug tests of athletes, because such tests are mandatory only for those who choose to participate in those voluntary activities.[12]

A few years later in 1998, the Rush County School District adopted a policy that required random urinalysis of all students who participated in extracurricular activities, not just athletics. In addition, the policy included tests for nicotine and alcohol. The policy also authorized testing all students who drove to school. The court immediately threw out the testing of those who drive to school but said, "We find the reasoning compelling drug testing of athletes also applies to testing of students in extracurricular activities. Certainly extracurricular activities require healthy students."[13]

Another area of privacy concerns student records. At one time teachers were required to write explicit statements concerning various student matters, such as a student's behavior, attitudes, actions, and even hygiene, from a belief that such information would be useful in working with the student in the future. These comments were considered to be private, in that they were shared only among educators working with the student. However, such records often were made available rather freely to outside agencies. Such information, often based on opinion rather than fact, could embarrass the student or cast a student in an unfavorable light, which might affect a future job or college placement.

Consider these commonplace examples of statements from students' cumulative record folders:

"This girl is a thief and a liar — do not trust her at all."

"Do not paddle on the posterior; student may defecate on himself."

"A lost year — student does little or no work."

Which of these statements violates a student's privacy rights? Quite simply, the answer is: All of them.

Fortunately, requirements for teachers to place such comments on file were changed by the 1974 Family Educational Rights and Privacy Act, also know as FERPA or the Buckley Amendment. However, teachers and administrators can still run afoul of this statute.

FERPA governs privacy issues in public schools largely by requiring any institution that receives public funds to allow parents to review the records written about their children. Parents can — and often do — object to biased comments about their children and demand that such comments be removed.

Furthermore, the act adds that schools can release such records to other agencies and individuals only with written permission of the parents, though there are some exceptions to this rule. Not all education records are protected, but certain items are, including medical information, special education status, test results, and similar private matters.

The key in court cases involving privacy issues is whether parents and students had legitimate expectations of privacy. The *Restatement (Second) of Torts* lists four different items that are considered as invading privacy:

- Intrusion upon seclusion.
- Appropriation of name or likeness.
- Publicity given to private life.
- Publicity placing a person in a false light.

Teachers or other school officials who do any of these things may be liable for invasion of privacy. For example, if a school newsletter discloses a distressing private fact about a student — that the student was adopted, for example — then the student may sue for invasion of privacy. This example would fall under the "publicity given to private life" standard.

Two cases illustrate privacy problems before FERPA. An Alabama case revealed that disciplinary actions against students were inaccurate and damaging. Some black students were placed on probation or expelled for civil rights demonstrations. The reason for expulsion was not explained in the records. The court ruled that students have sufficiently strong liberty and property interests to know their records.[14]

A second case determined that parents have a right to examine their children's records to prevent school abuse of the interests of handicapped children.[15]

The Constitution does not contain any specific reference to the right of privacy; but as the examples in this chapter show, a number of court cases have guaranteed that right. As an arm of government, public schools must meet certain due process and reasonable search-and-seizure requirements with regard to property and privacy rights of students (and parents). Schools that violate these requirements jeopardize their federal (and sometimes state) funding and may face legal actions.

It may sound silly for a teacher to be sued for trespass for tearing up something as trivial as a student's comic book, but such a suit could ask for punitive damages on the basis of the embarrassment that the incident caused the student. Property and privacy laws still are changing in education. The Constitution and various federal laws set a framework for these issues, but state statutes, state constitutions, and common law also come into play.

Notes

1. Jennings v. Joshua Independent School District, 877 F.2d 313 (5th Cir. 1989).
2. New Jersey v. T.L.O., 469 U.S. 325 (1985).
3. Bellnier v. Lund, 438 F. Supp. 47 (N.D.N.Y. 1977).
4. Widener v. Frye, 809 F. Supp. 35 (S.D. Ohio 1992).
5. Commonwealth v. Carey, 554 N.E.2d 1199 (Mass. 1990).
6. State v. Brooks, 718 P.2d 837 (Wash. App. 1986).
7. People v. Corey, 250 Cal. Rptr. 359 (Cal. App. 1988).
8. State v. Slattery, 787 P.2d 932 (Wash. 1990).
9. Horton v. Goose Creek Indep. Sch. Dist., 690 F.2d 470 (5th Cir. 1982).
10. Anable v. Ford, 653 F. Supp. 22 (W.D. Ark. 1985), *modified*, 663 F. Supp. 149 (W.D. Ark. 1985).
11. Odenheim v. Carlstadt-East Rutherford Regional School Dist., 500 A.2d 709 (N.J. 1985).
12. Vernonia School District 47J v. Acton, 115 S. Ct. 2386 (1995).
13. Todd v. Rush County Schools, 133 F.3d 984 (7th Cir. 1998).
14. Dixon v. Alabama State Board of Education, 294 F.2d 150 (1964).
15. Miles v. Board of Education of the District of Columbia, 384 F. Supp. 866, 872 (1972).

Chapter Eight

CONFIDENTIALITY AND REPORTING REQUIREMENTS

Susan has a great deal of confidence in her math teacher, Ms. Smith. She says to her one day, "I need to talk to you, but first you must promise never to tell anyone." She then tells Ms. Smith how her uncle, who is in jail, is making her father run an illegal operation from their home. Susan says she is afraid of all the weird people coming to the house. How should Ms. Smith handle this information? Is she obligated by the student's confidence in her to say nothing? Or is she obligated to tell the principal or the police about the student's fears? Is there potential in this situation for child abuse?

In Chapter Seven I touched on privacy issues with regard, in particular, to student records. Most student records must be regarded as confidential — that is, for the eyes of only students, their parents, and designated school officials. However, privacy is related in general to confidentiality issues, which also arise in other areas.

Confidentiality and privileged communication center on three questions: 1) Can a teacher tell a third party damaging information about a student? 2) Is information provided to a teacher confidential or privileged? 3) If a teacher is called into court, must the teacher relay that information?

"Privileged communication" is accorded to physicians in relation to their patients, attorneys in relation to their clients, priests in confession in relation to their penitents, and married persons in relation to their spouses. Certainly, students may confide in a teacher they trust. However, if the teacher accepts the role of confidant, he or she cannot guarantee the student that everything said will remain confidential. If the teacher is called to court, he or she can be required to testify and reveal the information exchanged. This also is true for school counselors. Privileged communication is afforded to licensed clinical psychologists but not to school counselors.

In the example, Ms. Smith needs to take several actions. First, she needs to let Susan know that, while she may be able to keep what Susan says just between the two of them, there is no guarantee of that. If Ms. Smith were subpoenaed, she would have to tell the court what Susan said.

Second, Ms. Smith may need to report Susan's remarks because of two factors. The first is suspicion of illegal activity; the second is the potential for child abuse. Both reports take precedence over confidentiality in the teacher-student relationship.

Reporting illegal activity relating to students both in and out of school is binding upon teachers. For example, if you are at a party where a host is serving alcohol to minors, you must let the host know that this is an illegal activity. One union representative in Michigan told teachers that failure to do so could cause them to be fired immediately.

Defamation

Educators must be aware of the potential for defamation. I mentioned a similar problem (invasion of privacy) in relation to written records and the need to keep them confidential. But the same cautions apply to verbal exchanges. Information that places students in a negative light can be relayed to other school personnel, such as a counselor, administrator, or social worker. But such exchanges must have a professional basis; casual conversation (as in a faculty lounge, for example) is inappropriate for this type of information exchange.

If such information is conveyed "beyond the school walls" and a student's character is thereby impugned, then the student (and his or her parents) may have cause to bring suit for defamation.

Educators also must be careful not to step beyond the boundaries of their own competence or expertise. For example, most teachers are not qualified to evaluate a student's personality or to diagnose a psychological disorder. Referring to a student as "schizophrenic" or "manic depressive" may seem like a shorthand way of describing the student's behavior, but in fact such clinical terms are being applied without a sound basis. If such characterizations are made public, they may be seen as damaging and, therefore, may be reasons to bring suit for defamation.

Child Abuse Reporting

Alexander and Alexander write: "While the phenomena of child abuse and neglect are ageless, only recently have they been given national attention."[1] That national attention actually began more than 30 years ago, in 1974, when Congress passed the Child Abuse Prevention and Treatment Act (P.L. 93-147), which provided financial assistance to states that implemented programs to prevent child abuse. Since that time, all 50 states, the District of Columbia, Puerto Rico, and the Virgin Islands have enacted statutes requiring the reporting of child abuse.

The definitions of child abuse and neglect vary widely among those laws. For example, some state laws include malnutrition or lack of proper clothing or dental care as abuse, while others do not. What is common to all of the laws is the requirement that educators report abuse or suspected abuse. "Suspected abuse" is a key phrase; abuse need not be proven to be reportable. Failure to report suspected child abuse can result in criminal charges of negligence being filed against the educator, may make the educator liable for the injuries that result from abuse, and can result in a fine (up to $1,000), a prison term (as much as one year), or disciplinary action by the school board.

Florida appears to have an inordinate number of child abuse cases, or it may be the situations are so egregious that they generate a lot of publicity. In Citrus County in March 2005, ten-year-old Jessica Lunsford was raped and buried alive clutching her little purple dolphin. Her death was from asphyxiation. A subcontracted mason, who had worked at Jessica's school, confessed to the crime. Because of this, the Florida Legislature passed the Jessica Lunsford Act requiring any person who comes on campus and has contact with kids to have a background check and be fingerprinted. In a regular school, a large number of people come on school campuses; substitutes, volunteers, maintenance contractors, even vendors of rings and year books, are just a few examples.

In my district, two teachers on car duty noticed a parent waiting to pick up her child. The parent stumbled around her car, then climbed into the car to sleep. Suspecting that the parent has been drinking or using drugs, the teachers refused to put the child in the car. An administrator came and put the child into the car, and the mother swerved off to pick up her son, who was at a middle school three miles away. The administrator then called the school resource officer at the middle school, who intercepted the mother at the school. A test showed that the mother had a blood alcohol level of 2.6.

At first it appears that the administrator did the right thing: calling the resource officer to intercept the mother and administer the drug test. However, what would have happened if the mother had an accident while driving to the middle school and the child was killed or injured? What responsibility would the administrator bear?

By letting the child get into the car, the administrator was endangering that child and could be guilty of child abuse. The administrator could have had her license suspended.

The signs of abuse are sometimes difficult to spot. Most teachers know that if a child comes to class bruised or scratched, they should suspect abuse. However, what about the following example?

A fourth-grade teacher at a rural elementary school noticed a terrible smell around the seat of a student. The boy had defecated in his pants. When sent to the office, he thought it was funny. The same thing happened again two more times. School administrators called parents, psychologists, and others to help diagnose the boy's problems. The boy relished the attention and laughed at the questions that were asked him. Was the boy seeking attention, or was this a sign of some other problem?

This condition, called *encopesis*, is a major red flag for sexual abuse. The child usually thinks it is funny and is encouraged to continue by getting so much attention. There are many other signs and symptoms that educators need to know.

All states grant civil and criminal immunity from libel or slander actions on the basis of reports of suspected child abuse that are made in good faith, even if the suspected abuse cannot be proved. For example, in an Oregon case a teacher reported suspected child abuse. When the abuse charge could not be proved, the parents sued the teacher. The court ruled that the teacher was immune from such a legal action because the report of suspected child abuse was made in good faith.[2]

Corporal Punishment: Child Abuse?

Is a teacher or principal who paddles a child in a state that permits paddling guilty of abuse? With the increasing emphasis on preventing child abuse, most states and school districts have become uncomfortable with allowing corporal punishment. Paddling has been outlawed in many states, and many school districts in states that statutorily permit paddling now forbid corporal punishment in their jurisdictions.

Educators who contemplate the use of corporal punishment must be aware of the applicable state laws and their school board's policies on such punishment. Even when paddling is permitted, care must be taken to follow the laws and policies to the letter and to exercise restraint. Excessive force may be claimed if insufficient consideration is given to the punished student's size, age, strength, and other physical factors. (See section in Chapter 6 on corporal punishment.)

A number of states and municipalities maintain registries of abusers. The courts may uphold the placing of educators' names on such lists if their use of corporal punishment is deemed to be excessive.

Confidentiality and reporting requirements can sometimes seem to be at odds. It is important for all educators to learn what can and cannot be said or written, what must be held in confidence or shared only professionally, and what must be reported. The information in this chapter is merely a starting point for consideration of these issues; more information must be obtained through school district policies and the laws in various localities.

Notes

1. Kern Alexander and M. David Alexander, *American Public School Law*, 3d ed. (St. Paul, Minn.: West, 1992), p. 313.
2. McDonald v. State of Oregon, 694 P.2d 569 (Or. App. 1985); *rev. denied*, 698 P.2d 964 (Or. 1985).

Chapter Nine

SPECIAL EDUCATION LAW

In the past, children with disabilities were invisible, throwaway kids. There were a few advocates for children with special needs in the early 19th century. In 1817 in Hartford, Connecticut, Thomas Gallaudet founded the earliest school for students with disabilities, then called the American Asylum for the Education of the Deaf and Dumb, now the American School for the Deaf. In 1832, New York established a school for blind students, and by 1852, New York, Pennsylvania, and Massachusetts had appropriated money for retarded children.

But other children had difficulty conforming to the requirements and structure of public schools, and law cases did not help them. An 1893 Massachusetts court ruled that imbecility was grounds for expulsion.[1] A Wisconsin court ruled that a student with a disability was capable but could be excluded from public schools because "his disability had a depressing and nauseating effect on the teachers and school children."[2] Thus children with cerebral palsy or poliomyelitis were prevented from attending public schools.

A turning point came when many soldiers returned from World War I with disabilities. The Soldiers' Rehabilitation Act and Smith-Bankhead Act offered vocational services in the form of counseling and training. By 1944, these acts were amended to include mentally retarded and mentally ill persons. But one of the most important decisions turned out to be the *Brown* v. *Board of Education* desegregation order of 1954. In mandating the rights of black children, the scene was set to include access to education for all children, including those with disabilities.[3]

In 1971 a Pennsylvania court determined that retarded children in Pennsylvania are entitled to a free, public education.[4] The ruling stated that whenever possible, retarded children must be educated in a regular classroom, rather than being segregated from normal school populations. In 1972 the *Mills* v. *Board of Education of District of Columbia* decision included all children with disabilities. This case mandated the three following provisions:

- A free appropriate public education (FAPE).
- An individualized education program (IEP).
- Due process procedures.[5]

The language and ideas of these two cases were included in the Education for All Handicapped Children Act (EAHCA) in 1975. That act required a free appropriate public education for all children with disabilities. Since that time, EAHCA has been amended numerous times, each time reaffirming the original intent. Three statutes establish procedural safeguards that must be followed:

- Individuals with Disabilities Education Act (IDEA)
- Section 504 of the Rehabilitation Act of 1973
- Americans with Disabilities Act of 1990

Individuals with Disabilities Education Act (IDEA)

In order to receive services, a child must have a qualifying disability and the condition must have an effect on that individual's education to the extent that it requires delivery of special education programs and related services. EAHCA was renamed the Individuals with Disabilities Education Act in 1990, and a few new provisions were added. In 1997 IDEA was amended to affect eligibility, programming, private school placements, discipline, funding, attorney's fees, discipline resolution, and procedural safeguards; but it did not change the general definition of a child with a disability. IDEA caused lots of confusion in the local districts, which demanded clarification of the many vague and conflicting provisions.

On 3 December 2004, the president signed the Individuals with Disabilities Education Improvement Act of 2004 (IDEA 2004), the final bill reauthorizing IDEA 1997. This act changes how many services are provided to students but does not change the districts' basic obligation to provide FAPE. Most provisions became effective 1 July 2005.[6] Following is a summary of the changes:

Changes in the District's Disciplinary Authority. The manifestation determination review (MDR), which is the hearing to determine whether the student's disability had a causal relationship to the misconduct, will need to ask only the two following questions: Did the disability cause the conduct? and Did the district's failure to implement the IEP cause the misconduct? If the answer to either of these questions is "yes," then the misconduct was a disability manifestation.

Under the old rule, there were four questions. Many observers believe that the two questions will be less likely than the older questions to find that a student's misconduct was a manifestation of the student's disability.

Under the new rules, the district will be able to use 45-day interim alternative placements for students who cause serious bodily injury. Previously, this option was available only for drug and weapons offenses. Also, the time was extended from 45 days to 45 school days. Now the district may remove the student from the classroom and place the student in an alternative setting during the appeals process. Previously, the "stay-put" provision barred the alternative placement during the appeal.

Writing and Changing IEPs. Districts no longer will have to include benchmarks and short-term objectives in IEPs, but they will have to describe how the student's progress toward annual goals will be measured. The IEP states when those progress reports will be made, such as quarterly or with report cards. The Education Department may publish models for IEPs that have individualized family service plans, procedural safeguards, and notices.

A parent may agree to modify the IEP in writing without another formal meeting. An IEP team member may be excused if the district and parents agree the member's services are not needed, or the team member may submit written input before the meeting. The staff may use alternative meetings, such as videoconferences and conference calls. Also, the Education Department may give up to 15 states the privilege to develop multiple-year IEPs that would last as long as three years.

Evaluating Students. The staff has more options if parents refuse consent. Although parental agreement is still an important part of the process, IDEA 2004 permits some initial evaluations — in certain circumstances — without parental consent. Unless state law demands parental consent, the district may do an evaluation, but it still must follow all procedural safeguards. In addition, if the parent does not consent, the district will not be liable for failing to convene an IEP meeting, failing to develop an IEP, and not providing special education and related services.

Identifying Specific Learning Disabilities. Under IDEA 1997, the district was required to ask the question: Is there a severe discrepancy between the student's achievement and his or her intellectual ability? IDEA 2004 allows districts to use a process that determines whether the student responds to scientific, research-based intervention. Thus educators have more flexibility in categorizing a student with a learning disability, even if he does not meet the former criteria for learning disabilities.

Student Transfers. Because of a lot of confusion, new IDEA language follows existing case law and says that students who transfer during a school year from one district to another within the same state must receive comparable services until the old IEP is adopted or a new one is developed. If students transfer from out of state, the district must conduct a new evaluation and then develop a new IEP; however, until the district conducts this evaluation, it must provide services comparable to what the child received before transferring.

Due Process Hearings. To discourage litigation, new provisions limit the time within which due process hearings may be requested. Parents have two years from the date they know about the issues for due process. In the past, state law established the time limit. In hopes of resolving complaints before they go to a formal hearing, an alternative dispute resolution (ADR) must be heard within 15 days to try to settle the matter.

Under IDEA 1997, parents who prevailed in due process cases were allowed to seek attorney's fees from the district; but if the district won, the district could not pursue these fees. Under current law, the following circumstances determine if the district may be awarded attorney's fees:

- The due process request or lawsuit is frivolous, unreasonable, or without foundation.
- The attorney continued to litigate after the litigation clearly became frivolous.
- The due process request or lawsuit was filed for the wrong purpose, such as harassment, unnecessary delays, or needlessly increasing the cost of litigation.

If the parents filed the suit for an improper purpose, then a district may be awarded the attorney's fees against that parent.

IDEA 2004 has new standards for highly qualified teachers that coincide with standards in the No Child Left Behind Act (NCLB). All teachers must be certified or licensed in special education, and anyone hired after July 2005 must meet the requirement. IDEA 2004 appears to offer flexibility on the point of certification: Teachers at an elementary level must meet the highly qualified provisions for an elementary school level, rather than standards for those of middle and high school students. Experienced special education teachers who teach two or more academic subjects may meet the highly qualified criteria by passing a single, multi-subject, state test.

Full funding of IDEA is a goal, but it still is not mandatory and falls short in congressional budgets. However, districts and states now may use their funds for some new uses, including:

- Supplemental educational services (SES) that provide technical assistance and direct service, but only for those districts that need improvement in the performance of the students in the disabilities subgroup.
- Districts may use up to 15% of the funds for early intervention services to students who have not yet been identified as disabled.
- States may set aside 10% of their state-level funds to create a risk pool that would help districts pay for students with high-cost needs or for unexpected spikes in enrollment of students with disabilities.

Much of the litigation involving special education cases arises from teachers and administrators not knowing the law. Court cases relating to special education are varied, but they fall into the following groups:

- Free appropriate public education
- Procedural safeguards
- Individualized education program
- Least restrictive environment
- Separate school placement
- Related services
- Discipline and a "stay-put" provision
- Attorney's fees
- Tuition reimbursement
- Special rules for 11 specific conditions

Many court cases have arisen as disputes between districts and parents. The district loses when it skirts due process or claims that it cannot perform a service because of the cost. For the courts, the cost of services is not an issue. Parents lose when they bring frivolous and unreasonable cases.

However, no issue causes more misunderstanding than that of disciplining special education students. The National School Boards Association has published the following guidelines:[7]

- For disciplinary reasons, schools may remove a student with a disability to an interim alternative education setting, another setting, or suspension for not more than 10 days in a school year. This short-term removal does not mean a change in placement. A series of short-term removals from the current placement that accumulate to more than 10 school days may require action by the IEP team for a 45-day placement. For drugs or weapon violations, the student may receive an alternative interim placement if the due process hearing officer determines that the school district has demonstrated that the child may cause injury to himself or to others. However, the alternative interim setting must provide the student with a free, appropriate public education.

- When removing students for more than 10 days, the discussion must begin by answering the two questions about whether the student's disability had a causal relationship to the misconduct. If the behavior was not related to the disability, disciplinary procedures applicable to those without disabilities are applied, except that the disabled child must continue to receive FAPE.

Another issue causing much litigation is *inclusion*. The IDEA requires that states, "to the maximum extent appropriate . . . educate children with disabilities . . . with children who are not disabled." This preference for mainstreaming is the basis of inclusion. The same section also provides that "special classes, separate schooling, or other removal of children with disabilities from the regular educational environment occurs only when the nature or severity of the disability is such that education in regular classes with the use of supplementary aids and services cannot be achieved satisfactorily."[8]

In 1983 *Roncker* v. *Walter* cited three factors to be considered in inclusion:

1. The comparative benefits of the two placements.
2. Any disruption by the student in the non-segregated setting.
3. The cost of mainstreaming the students.[9]

The Fourth and Eighth Circuits have adopted these factors as a test of inclusion. However, in 1989 the Fifth Circuit Court heard a case brought by the parents of a six-year old boy with Down Syndrome and a developmental age of two to three years. The parents wanted the child to be mainstreamed. The district argued for a different placement because, in prekindergarten, the child required constant attention from the teacher and could not master any of the skills being taught. The court rejected the *Roncker* test as too intrusive an inquiry into the state's education policy choices and developed the now-famous two-part test:

1. Can education in the regular classroom, with the use of supplementary aids and services, be achieved satisfactorily? If not, has the school mainstreamed the student to the maximum extent appropriate?
2. The following factors must be considered: steps to accommodate the child in the regular classroom, whether the child would receive educational benefit in the regular classroom, the child's overall experience in the regular classroom, and the effect of the child's presence on others in the regular classroom.[10]

There has yet to be a Supreme Court case on the issue of inclusion, but lower court decisions demonstrate the developing trend.

Section 504

Section 504 prohibits districts that receive federal funds from discriminating in the delivery of school programs and activities. This section differs from IDEA in that it is broader and is intended to prevent discrimination against students with disabilities. The definition of a disability under 504 has three parts:

1. Student has a physical or mental impairment. This is not limited to the 11 classifications under IDEA. For example, the team should not require parents to provide a medical

diagnosis and can use qualified school personnel with appropriate training to determine eligibility.

2. The impairment must limit a major life activity. Unlike IDEA, this is not limited to learning. Courts have interpreted the meaning in global terms and require that the student have a history of such impairment. Thus students with communicable diseases, diabetes, ADHD, asthma, or allergies may qualify.

3. The frame of reference is the average student in the general population. The limitation is substantial if the child cannot do things that the average child of the same age can do. Norm-referenced standardized test data may be useful in determining this relation to the average student.[11]

Section 504 seeks to remove hurdles to participation in schools, whether to such physical barriers as a wheelchair or in program barriers that exclude a child.

Perry Zirkel states that eligibility and services have increased in recent years for the following reasons:

- The push in some areas to reduce identification of students under IDEA has increased pressure for 504/ADA coverage.
- The stigma associated with special education under IDEA and the lack of response in regular education has increased 504 plans.
- Survival in the new high-stakes environment for promotion or diplomas and the push for competitive advantage in tests for college admission have encouraged this direction.
- The collective accountability requirements of NCLB have captured the attention of parents and school leaders. Students under 504 plans do not count as part of the disaggregated group of students with disabilities.[12]

Americans with Disabilities Act

Title II of the Americans with Disabilities Act (ADA), which became effective 26 January 1992, prohibits discrimination in services, programs, and activities provided by state and local governments. Schools must make programs available and accessible to all disabled individuals who are otherwise qualified to participate in the program. A district may justify why programs are not fully available with the following defenses:

- Participation would cause a health or safety risk to the person or to others.
- Participation would require modification that would alter the program, services, or activities.
- Modification would result in undue financial or administrative burden.
- The requested device or service is personal in nature — for example, eye glasses or a hearing aid.

Figure 2. Differences in IDEA, Section 504, and ADA.		
IDEA	**Section 504**	**ADA**
Applies only if districts accept federal money.	Prohibits discrimination only in federally assisted programs and activities.	Applies to school districts regardless of federal funding.
Imposes more extensive obligations than ADA.		
Applies only to those children with disabilities in need of special education and related services.		
Only a court may award fees; they cannot be awarded for services that relate to IEP meeting except under limited circumstances.		Makes clear attorney's fees are available for legal services provided during administrative phase of proceeding and allows hearing officers to award them.
	Allows schools to take disciplinary action against students with disabilities who engage in illegal drugs or alcohol in same manner as students without disabilities.	Imposes an accommodation standard more stringent than in early cases interpreting 504.

However, the district must be aware that judges are concerned that the student will receive access to free and appropriate education. For example, Amber Tatro, an eight-year-old girl who was born with spina bifida, required catheterization every three or four hours. Her parents wanted her to receive those services at school. The court determined that a lay person with an hour's training could perform this procedure and ordered the district to provide this service.[13]

IDEA, Section 504, and the ADA all cover students with disabilities and place legal obligations on schools. The similarities and differences between these acts can be confusing. Figure 2 compares some of the major features of these acts.

The laws concerning special education have led educators to do what they have not done on their own. While problems still exist, we have come a long way in a short time.

Notes

1. Watson v. City of Cambridge, 157 Mass. 561, 32 N.E. 864 (1893).
2. State *ex.rel.* Beattie v. Board of Education, 169 Wis. 231, 172 N.W. (1919).
3. Brown v. Board of Education, 347 U.S. 483 (1954).
4. Pennsylvania Ass'n for Retarded Children v. Commonwealth, 334 F. Supp. 1257 (E.D. Pa. 1971), and 343 F. Supp. 279 (E.D. Pa. 1972).
5. Mills v. Board of Education of District of Columbia, 348 F. Supp. 866 (D.C. 1972).
6. Some information in the following section is adapted from *School Superintendent's Insider*, "Use Quick Reference Guide to IDEA Reauthorization Provisions," April 2005.
7. Ibid.
8. Ibid.
9. Roncker v. Walter, 700 F.2d 1058 (6th Cir. 1983).
10. Daniel R.R. v. State Board of Education, 874 F.2d 1036 (5th Cir. 1989).
11. Perry A. Zirkel, *Section 504: Student Issues, Legal Requirements, and Practical Recommendations* (Bloomington, Ind: Phi Delta Kappa Educational Foundation, 2005).
12. Ibid.
13. Irving Independent School District v. Tatro, 468 U.S. 883 (1984).

Chapter Ten

THE NO CHILD LEFT BEHIND ACT

The No Child Left Behind Act (NCLB) was enacted as part of the reauthorization of the Elementary and Secondary Education Act of 1965. The purpose of the act is "to ensure that ALL children have a fair, equal, and significant opportunity to obtain a high-quality education and reach, at a minimum, proficiency on challenging State academic achievement standards and State academic assessments."[1] Programs that were funded as part of this act include: Reading First, Even Start, Improving Literacy Through School Libraries, Education of Migratory Children, prevention and intervention programs for youth who are neglected, delinquent, or at-risk, school drop-out prevention programs, and school improvement/school reform.

The provisions of the act are complex and controversial. But the basic features of the act are outlined below:

- Each state must set aside at least 2% of NCLB grants for its lowest-achieving schools with the greatest need.
- State plans must be coordinated with IDEA and other federal programs.
- States must adopt standards of what children are expected to know and be able to do. Courses must contain coherent and rigorous content and encourage the teaching of advanced skills.
- States must develop and implement a single statewide accountability system that uses sanctions and rewards to ensure adequate yearly progress.

- Adequate yearly progress (AYP) requires schools to apply the same high standards of achievement to all public schools. All students must make continuous progress on measurable objectives for each subgroup — children with disabilities, economically disadvantaged students, students from major racial and ethnic groups, and students with limited English proficiency. Each state defines AYP with measurable objectives.
- States must ensure that not later than 12 years after the end of the 2001-2002 school year, all students in each group will meet or exceed the proficient levels of academic achievement on statewide tests.
- AYP includes baseline data, annual measurable objectives, and intermediate goals applied to all the subgroups. Every year each subgroup must meet or exceed the annual objectives of the state.
- At least 95% of students in each group are required to take the statewide assessments in reading, mathematics, and science. Failure to test at least 95% of children with disabilities automatically results in failure to make AYP. Up to 1% of students with disabilities may be given an alternative assessment that measures these children's achievement toward their appropriate academic standards.
- Students with disabilities will receive "reasonable adaptations and accommodations necessary to measure achievement relative to state academic standards."
- LEP students must be assessed in a valid and reliable manner and provided reasonable accommodation in the language and form most likely to yield accurate data.
- Each state must prepare a state report card, reporting aggregated test data on student achievement at each proficiency level and also disaggregated test data for subgroups based on race/ethnicity, migrant status, gender, disability, English proficiency, and students who are economically disadvantaged. The only exception is where the number of students in a subgroup is insufficient to yield statistically reliable

information. The data must be available to the local education agency (LEA) before the beginning of the year.

- Parents have a right to know. At the beginning of the school year, the LEA must notify parents about the following professional qualifications of the student's teachers: whether the teacher has met state qualification, whether the teacher is teaching under an emergency certificate or other waiver, post-secondary degrees held by the teacher, and qualifications of any paraprofessionals that may be assigned to room.
- All districts must implement scientifically based, empirically validated instructional programs; but parents do not have the right to demand a particular choice of methodology. The programs must involve rigorous data analyses that involve experimental and quasi-experimental designs.

The consequences for failing to comply with NCLB are drastic. If the school fails for two consecutive years to make AYP as defined by the state, then all students have the option to transfer to another school. Priority is given to the lowest-achieving schools and students from low-income families. After the fifth year of corrective action, some specific actions may be taken:

- Give up Title I grants.
- School choice is continued, and parents may choose another school.
- Reopen as a charter school.
- Replace all or most of the staff.
- Contract with a private agency to run the school.
- Turn the LEA over to the state.
- Other major restructuring strategy.

One of the most questionable provisions is the requirement of highly qualified teachers and paraprofessionals. All teachers hired after the enactment of NCLB (January 2002) who are teaching core academic subjects must be fully certified to teach those subjects. All teachers who were teaching prior to the enactment of NCLB were required to become highly qualified by the end of the 2005-2006 year.

Results of the 2005 Phi Delta Kappa International/Gallup poll indicate that most Americans do not know a lot about NCLB. While most people approve of the idea of accountability, the details of the laws are quite messy, especially when various states interpret and set up their own qualifications. Paul Houston, executive director of the American Association of School Administrators, said that the poll offers good news and bad news for educators. "Members of the public want to see the achievement gap closed and understand that the gap is created outside the schools, but they believe schools can overcome the ravages of social and economic conditions. . . . these expectations could set the schools up for failure if they *cannot* do what society *will* not do."[2]

Some provisions of NCLB undoubtedly will be tried in the courts. On 13 April 2005 Connecticut became the first state to announce that it was challenging the law, mostly on the ground that the law was an unfunded mandate that was placed on the states for implementation. The NEA filed a previous suit in U.S. District Court in Detroit. Joining that suit were the districts of Pontiac, Michigan, Laredo, Texas, and a cluster of rural districts outside Rutland, Vermont.[3] Virginia and Utah challenges are possible. More cases are probably out there, and what the final outcome will be is anybody's guess.

Notes

1. 20 U.S.C. Section 6301.
2. Lowell C. Rose and Alec M. Gallup "37th Annual Phi Delta Kappa/Gallup Poll of the Public's Attitudes Toward the Public Schools," *Phi Delta Kappan* 87 (September 2005): 41-63.
3. "NCLB Cases Face Hurdles in the Courts," *Education Week*, 4 May 2005. http://www.edweek.org/ew/articles/2005/05/04/34nclbsuits.h24.html?rale=14RcsgF70mPtC

Chapter Eleven

CHRONIC ILLNESS AND MEDICAL EMERGENCIES

A student with a history of asthma staggered out of an assembly at Lawless High School in New Orleans and told a school security guard that she was having trouble breathing. The guard called the assistant principal, who tried to contact the girl's mother to see if she would pay for an ambulance to transport the girl to the hospital.

Then the student was taken to the counselor's office, and the counselor also tried to reach the mother. After 34 minutes, the girl's 14-year-old sister called 911 herself. The stricken girl died before help arrived. In subsequent legal action the judge ruled that the principal had shirked his duty to protect the child from harm and awarded damages to the parents: $1.4 million from the named officials and $200,000 from the school board.

The attorney for the plaintiffs commented, "It was a tragedy of errors. These individuals didn't take things as seriously as they should have."[1]

Children with chronic illnesses and other problems have a right to participate in the normal activities of the school to the extent that they are able to do so. However, such students also have a right to concerned care.

Clearly, educators must be aware of the ramifications of chronic illness in order to avoid tragic situations like the one in this example. As a general rule, if a student claims to be ill, then he or she should be treated as if the claim were accurate, unless circumstances clearly dictate otherwise. If a medical emergency arises, the focus must be on doing what is best for the child. Stopping to consider who will pay, as in the example, is not a reasonable consideration in a medical emergency.

One procedure that is helpful in avoiding problems related to chronic illness is for teachers to be aware of such conditions. Most schools require parents to complete registration forms that ask for information about their child's health. Counselors and teachers should review this information so that they know which students need to be monitored for signs of illness.

In the age of instant medical information, it is inexcusable for people not to know about diseases and disorders. If you know of a student who has a particular disease, try to find out as must as possible about that disease and apply that to classroom conditions. For example, a student with sickle cell anemia may have a painful episode in class. Knowing what may happen can help the teacher handle situations more comfortably. But be sure to use such reliable sources as medical personnel and such websites as webMD.com, www.medline.com, or www.cdc.gov, which offer reliable information. However, be aware that all websites are not equal and that misinformation abounds. Be especially wary of any sites that are trying to sell a product.

Of course, not all medical emergencies result from chronic illness. In an Illinois case, an 11-year-old was awarded $2.5 million in damages because the school failed to provide prompt medical assistance. The student suffered a head injury that resulted in a blood clot. School officials called the boy's parents, who authorized them to take the child to the hospital across the street from the school. The school called for an ambulance, which took a full hour to arrive. During that time the blood clot swelled from the size of a walnut to the size of an orange. In the subsequent suit the court reasoned that, under the circumstances, the school should have taken the boy across the street to the hospital, rather than delaying in order to wait for an ambulance.[2]

In a medical emergency prompt action is essential. Delays sometimes can be deadly — and costly.

Emergency communication between school and home should be channeled through a designated staff member. In most schools this person is the principal or the school nurse. The telephone numbers needed to contact students' parents or guardians should be readily accessible for this purpose.

Chronic Illnesses

The general population has little knowledge of diseases and disorders, and misinformation, half-truths, or folk treatments abound. Unfortunately, school personnel fit in this category. Many educators have little knowledge of the disorders they may encounter and fail to recognize important symptoms that require action. One condition bathed with myths is epilepsy.

Epilepsy. Epilepsy is a general label for more than 20 types of seizures. With petit mal seizures, the child briefly blacks out; and a teacher may "fuss" at her for not paying attention. A child with simple partial or psychomotor seizures may get out of his seat and wander aimlessly around the classroom while pulling at sleeves or doing some unusual repetitive motion. An unaware teacher may think the child is seeking attention or on drugs. If a teacher observes such behavior, the child needs to be referred for evaluation.

Teachers need to know what to do if a student has a seizure. For example, during math class Eddie falls out of his chair. His body becomes very rigid and begins to shake. The teacher realizes that Eddie is experiencing some type of seizure. In addition to calling the office for help, what should the teacher do?

1. Restrain Eddie so that he cannot jerk around and hurt himself.
2. Put something into Eddie's mouth so that he will not swallow his tongue.
3. Move chairs and desks out of Eddie's way so that he does not hit them and injure himself.

Eddie's fall from his chair, body rigidity, and shaking are typical of an epileptic seizure. The appropriate response is 3: Move things out of Eddie's way and let the seizure run its course while help is being summoned. In most cases, once the seizure has passed, the individual will return to normal. Eddie may be embarrassed by the episode, and the seizure may leave him fatigued. He may need to go home or to the nurse's office to recover fully. Parents should be notified of the episode so that they can obtain medical advice. Epilepsy can be controlled by medication in most cases; however, Eddie may have skipped a dose. Or the dosage might need to be adjusted.

Asthma. About three million children under the age of 18 suffer from asthma, a complex disease that causes breathing passages to constrict. The case at the beginning of this chapter shows a school that completely mishandled a student with an attack, waiting to call the mother to see if she would pay for the ambulance to take the child to the hospital.

Diabetes. With the rise of obesity, cases of diabetes are increasing. This condition is one that teachers probably will encounter more often in the classroom. Teachers need to be aware that the most common times for low blood sugar reactions are just before lunch and in the middle of the afternoon. Generally, students have mid-morning and mid-afternoon snacks to avoid these episodes. The student may be very thirsty and ask to use the restroom more often. Physical education teachers need to be aware that participation in sports and exercise — while very important for diabetics — tends to lower blood sugar.

Educators may encounter numerous medical conditions, including juvenile arthritis, forms of cancer, cystic fibrosis, and others. For any of these health care issues, good communications involves forming a health care team that includes parents, the student, medical professionals, teachers, and administrators. Knowing what medications are used and that medications may cause side effects is exceedingly important. While educators may say they do not need another series of meetings, the importance cannot be underestimated. The question is: Can you afford not to have the meeting?

Communicable Diseases

Laws regarding communicable diseases are changing. Most students may be excluded from school during the period when they may infect others. For example, schools can exclude students who have measles or chicken pox. In most jurisdictions schools are required to notify health authorities of suspected cases of measles, rubella, pertussis, mumps, poliomyelitis, hepatitis B, or hemophilus influenza - type B. Health authorities also may declare communicable disease emergencies and remove children from school who are not immunized.

In recent years the automatic exclusion of students with communicable diseases has been reconsidered, largely as a result of the acquired immune deficiency syndrome (AIDS) epidemic. While the human immunodeficiency virus (HIV) that causes AIDS is communicable, the courts have held in several cases that school authorities cannot exclude infected students (or teachers), because there is no evidence of casual HIV transmission. (HIV is spread primarily through contact with infected blood or sexual contact with an infected person.)

As an example, in 1989 a court ruled that an incontinent, drooling, developmentally disabled child with AIDS could not be excluded from the classroom or denied educational services. The court held that casual contact with the student was not threatening to the health of the other students.[3]

The standard for communicable diseases, including HIV, is to assume that everyone is a potential carrier. The key principle of universal precaution is to avoid contact with another person's blood or body fluids. Teachers should have access to latex gloves to wear when attending scrapes, cuts, or nosebleeds at school. Playground supervisors should carry gloves in case of a mishap. If one does come in contact with another person's blood, immediately wash the contact area with soap and water. Blood spills should be cleansed with a mixture of nine parts water to one part bleach. Students also should be taught universal precautions.

Medication

School officials are not permitted to dispense medicines except under certain circumstances and only when proper authorizations have been given by parents or physicians. Gatti and Gatti provide the following guidelines from the American Academy of Pediatrics Committee on School Health:

1. School personnel are permitted to give students medicine, provided that a physician has supplied written instructions that detail the name of the medicine, the dosage to be administered, a schedule for medication, and a diagnosis or reason for medicating the student.
2. A parent or guardian must provide written permission for medicine to be dispensed, even in the case of nonprescription medicines.
3. Parents must supply medicines in the original container.
4. One school staff member should be designated as the dispenser, preferably a school nurse.
5. The school must keep medicines in a locked cabinet.
6. Communication between school and home (and physician, in some cases) should be maintained with regard to the effectiveness of the medication.[4]

Most schools have policies forbidding students to carry their own medicines; however, there are some exceptions. For example, students with chronic asthma may be permitted to carry a metered-dose inhaler. Parents of students with chronic asthma must provide a doctor's statement affirming the need for the student to have the inhaler in his or her possession, and they also should ensure that a spare inhaler is kept in the school's locked medicine cabinet.

State laws usually protect the school staff member who administers medications from liability for civil damages if that person follows exactly the school's policies — and any physician's instructions — and acts as any reasonable and prudent person would under similar circumstances. Indeed, "prudent action" is a standard of law.

First Aid

The responsibility to administer first aid goes beyond cases of chronic illness. Thus all teachers — especially in potentially hazardous teaching situations, such as industrial arts shops, cooking labs, art studios, gyms and playing fields, and so on — need basic training in first aid. If an emergency arises, educators can be held liable for failing to administer first aid.

For example, a 16-year-old boy in Louisiana collapsed after football practice. He displayed signs of heat stroke. However, the coach delayed obtaining medical treatment for the boy for nearly two hours. The boy never regained consciousness and died later that day. The coach was held liable for failure to give proper first aid and for failure to summon prompt medical attention.[5]

In the case of epilepsy and other chronic illnesses, a basic understanding of chronic conditions will be useful for all educators. This basic knowledge can guide in the application of first aid.

Suicide and Death

No one knows why a young person will take his or her own life, but the facts are startling. A 1991 World Health Organization study revealed that in the past 35 years, suicide among young people increased more than for other age groups: 300% for males and 230% for females. Some of these attempts may occur on school grounds. What responsibilities does the school have in these situations? In addition to concern, educators need to be vigilant and use the care of supervision that they would use with any situation.

For example, Jamie, a 14-year-old student, misbehaved in physical education class, and the teacher sent her to the locker room. While she was in the unsupervised locker room, she attempted suicide. Although she survived, she was permanently impaired. The parents sued the town, board of education, the superintendent, the school principal, and the gym teacher.

The court looked at a principle called "shock-the-conscience." Was the act of negligence so egregious that a person would be shocked about the conditions of the situation? The behavior must be one that must be malicious or seek to cause harm to Jamie in some way. The court ruled that the test might apply if the school had known that the child previously had threatened suicide or was a special education pupil not fully able to care for himself. Thus they ruled for the school district.[6]

In another case, a third-grade child hanged himself in a school bathroom with a length of nylon cord attached to a large plywood bathroom pass. The Arkansas Supreme Court said that a school cannot "shelter a growing child from every possible danger." They determined that the school had taken adequate safety measures and that it was "manifestly futile" to protect students from all possibilities of injury, self-inflicted or otherwise.[7]

Prudent Action

Educators do well to bear in mind the idea of "prudent action" when it comes to dealing with chronic illnesses, medical emergencies, the giving of medicines, and dealing with communicable diseases. Myrna Watkins, health supervisor in Marion County, Florida, offers the following guidelines for educators:[8]

- Educators should perform only first aid that is absolutely necessary. Most injuries at school are not life-threatening. If a child is bleeding or choking, then first aid may be necessary. But the proper response in many cases is simply to comfort the child until professional help arrives.
- School leaders should ensure that staff are trained in cardiopulmonary resuscitation (CPR). Some states require a certain number or percentage of a school's staff be trained, but training as many staff members as possible is prudent.
- Teachers need to be familiar with the chronic illnesses of students in their classrooms. Pertinent records should be

reviewed at the beginning of the year and periodically there-after to ensure up-to-date information about the health of students.

- Educators should act as a prudent parent would act in similar circumstances with regard to caring for students. They should not attempt procedures that they are not qualified to perform. (Example: A teacher who attempts to fix a dislocated shoulder may make the injury worse — and be liable for "playing doctor.")

- Schools should obtain emergency response checklists from their local health department or similar agency in order to have a ready reference for first aid. Such checklists can be helpful to have in every classroom.

- Paraprofessionals also should be trained in first aid and other emergency procedures, particularly if they are assigned to supervise students, such as during student playground time or while loading or unloading school buses.

- School leaders should ensure that safety precautions are observed in potentially hazardous classrooms and during activities that may result in injury. For example, students (and teachers) should be required to wear protective eyewear when working with certain tools or heating glass during a science experiment. Fire blankets should be available where conditions warrant, and so on.

- School personnel should be familiar with and observe the Universal Precautions recommended by the Centers for Disease Control and Prevention, such as donning rubber gloves before coming into contact with blood or other bodily fluids.

- School personnel should be advised not to give any form of medication to students, except as designated in accordance with school policy. Students should not be given aspirins, cough drops, or other seemingly innocuous, over-the-counter medications unless specific, written permission to do so has been given.

Educators who observe these guidelines are acting in a prudent manner and are unlikely to find themselves facing a liability suit as a result of improper response to a chronic illness or a medical emergency.

Notes

1. Jessica Portner, "Family Awarded 1.6 Million in Asthma Death at School," *Education Week*, 15 September 1996, p. 4.
2. Barth v. Board of Educ., 490 N.E.2d 77 (Ill. App. 1986).
3. Martinez v. Hillsborough County Sch. Bd., 711 F. Supp. 1066 (M.D. Fla. 1989).
4. Daniel J. Gatti and Richard D. Gatti, *The Educator's Encyclopedia of School Law* (Englewood Cliffs, N.J.: Prentice-Hall, 1990).
5. Mogabgab v. Orleans Parish Sch. Bd., 241 So. 2d 253 (La. Ct. App. 1970).
6. Hasenfus v. Lajeunesse, 175 F.3d 68 (1st Cir. 1999).
7. Gathright v. Lincoln Insurance Co., 286 Ark. 16, 688 S.W. 931 (1985).
8. Interview with Myrna Watkins, supervisor of health, Marion County, Florida, 4 November 2005.

Chapter Twelve

SEXUAL MISCONDUCT AND SEXUAL HARASSMENT

Scenes about sexual behavior are in the papers every day. I opened my morning paper and read of a female teacher who was accused of sex with a 12-year-old student of the same sex. Other cases of relationships with students make the newspapers and even the national news. Still, in spite of five unprecedented Supreme Court rulings — three involving sexual harassment in employment, one teacher-to-student harassment, and another on student-to-student or peer harassment — the incidents keep on coming.

Teachers and administrators too often bury their heads in the sand with an "it can't happen to me" attitude regarding sexual misconduct and sexual harassment. Consider the fate of a teacher I will call "Mr. L."

Mr. L had taught middle school art for 26 years. He was personable and friendly. Although he demanded high-quality work from his students, he also was well-liked. He patted students on the shoulder and encouraged them to do their best.

One October Mr. L was called into the principal's office and given the news that a female student had accused him of sexual misconduct. She said that Mr. L had patted her buttocks; and she had two witnesses, a boy and a girl. The girl's father was a police officer, who decided to press charges.

Over the next two years Mr. L was suspended, first with pay and then without, and his name was dragged through the local newspapers. Finally, the state's attorney general dropped the criminal charges; but the school board sanctioned Mr. L, placed him on an annual contract, and transferred him to an elementary school.

At the elementary school some parents now accuse Mr. L of being too demanding and making children cry. Some teachers at the school speculate that the parents are "out to get" Mr. L because of the previous incident.

Guilt or innocence is not necessarily the main issue in emotionally charged sexual misconduct and sexual harassment cases. Often an accusation alone is enough to irreparably damage an educator's career.

Issues of Morality

How schools (and the law) deal with sexual misconduct and sexual harassment issues in the school setting are a reflection of how society views sexual morality issues generally.

At one time it was common for schools to insist that female teachers remain unmarried. To marry was to lose one's position, a restriction not placed on male teachers. Indeed, male teachers were encouraged to marry, and family "breadwinners" were paid more than unmarried teachers. In 1923 the U.S. Supreme Court changed that in a ruling on personal freedom, which included "not merely freedom from bodily harm but also the right of the individual to. . . marry, to establish a home. . . and to enjoy those privileges. . . essential to the orderly pursuit of happiness of free men."[1]

In spite of this ruling and others, questions still arise with regard to school boards' rights versus the private rights of individuals over such matters as marriage, pregnancy, and sexual relations. The "spill-over" comes when teachers are charged with sexual misconduct and that alleged misconduct has taken place outside the school setting. At issue is whether a connection exists between conduct (or misconduct) outside the school and the ability of the individual to perform his or her professional duties.

For example, in a rural South Dakota case in 1976 a teacher was dismissed because people in the community complained that she was living openly with her boyfriend and refused to change her lifestyle. A federal appellate court held that the school's interest in maintaining its moral position outweighed her due process interests. The court said, "Ms. Sullivan's conduct violated local mores, [and] her students were aware of this. . . . Ms. Sullivan was shown to have generated deep affection from her students, increasing the probability of emulation."[2]

On the other hand, also in 1976, when an unwed pregnant teacher in Nebraska was dismissed from her mid-size city school system, that community expressed little interest. The board had dismissed the teacher without considering alternative ways of handling the situation, such as permitting her to take a leave of absence. The court found for the teacher in this case.[3]

Most litigation involving morality issues (often termed "fitness to teach") centers on issues of sexual activity (homosexual or heterosexual) and drug use. School boards generally have been required to show that private activities conducted outside the school setting are detrimental to teaching (or administration). As a rule, persons cannot be denied government employment on the basis of factors unconnected to that employment.

Homosexual conduct, for example, has been the subject in a number of dismissal lawsuits. In general the courts have held that homosexuality per se is not ground for dismissal, and gay men and lesbians cannot be discriminated against in hiring on the basis of their sexual orientation. At the same time, the U.S. Supreme Court held in 1986 that homosexual conduct (specifically, sodomy) is not protected by privacy rights found in the Constitution.[4] However, gay or lesbian educators cannot be dismissed simply because they are homosexual; school boards must demonstrate a rational nexus between private conduct and fitness to teach.

Sexual conduct between consenting adults is one thing, but sexual conduct between teachers and students, even outside the school setting, is indefensible. Privacy issues aside, such conduct is almost always considered inappropriate; and that is certainly the case when the students are minors.

Sexual Harassment

What is sexual harassment? In the simplest terms, sexual harassment consists of unwelcome sexual advances, requests for sexual favors, and other inappropriate oral, written, or physical conduct of a sexual nature such that the action interferes with an employee's work performance or with a student's education. Harassment may be student to student, teacher (or other school employee) to student or vice versa, employee to employee, or employer to employee. State laws vary with regard to sexual harassment among students. For example, in California only children in the fourth grade and older are included in the sexual harassment laws. However, in Minnesota even kindergartners can be expelled for repeated acts of harassment.

In a 1986 case, the Supreme Court recognized that severe and persistent harassment that included unwelcome sexual advances, abusive language, and demeaning behavior based on sex resulting in a hostile work environment, was actionable under Title VII. If the employers have known of the behavior and nothing is done, the victims do not have to sustain economic losses but can collect for psychological injuries.[5]

In addition to harassment of employees, schools also must face cases of sexual harassment of students by teachers or other students. The example that opened this chapter demonstrates how a career can be ruined by such allegations even if the teacher is not formally charged with a crime.

Actions are always open to interpretation — and misinterpretation. Consider the case of a middle school teacher in Missouri. In a burst of enthusiasm, a male teacher hugged and kissed a male eighth-grade student in a school corridor. The student was shocked and interpreted the teacher's action as a "pass," which he reported to the principal. The teacher explained that the action was simply natural enthusiasm, that such expressions were common in his family, and that no sexual content was intended.

The school board fired the teacher, who then brought suit. His firing was upheld by the lower court; but the appeals court overturned that ruling, saying that the school board had no policy on sexual harassment and had failed to show intentional misconduct. The reaction by the student did not turn a well-intended act into an immoral one. Thus the appeals court ordered the school board to reinstate the teacher.[6]

The point in this illustration does not turn on the question of "to hug or not to hug." Rather, the point is: Does the school board have a reasonable policy regarding conduct that may be construed as sexual harassment?

Student-to-student sexual harassment also is a serious issue for schools. For example, Lashonda Davis, a Georgia fifth-grade student, complained to her teacher that another student, GF, had made such vulgar statements as "I want to get in bed with you," and "I want to feel your boobs." The teacher reported it to the principal. The next month, Lashonda reported the incident to her mother, who called the teacher. Later, GF proceeded to act in a sexually suggestive manner during a physical education class. No action was taken. A string of incidents continued, but the school took no action. The school board had no policy on peer harassment nor had staff been trained on how to handle problems.

The federal district court dismissed the complaint, but the 11th Circuit Court of Appeals reversed the dismissal, and the case went to the Supreme Court. The Supreme Court was very disturbed at the school's indifferent handling of the situation. The Court clarified that it did not expect districts to expel every student accused of harassing peers or to grant a stipend to every victim. It did clarify that districts should have policies on harassment and to take allegations seriously.[7]

Legislation on sexual harassment has been in place since the passage of Title VII of the Civil Rights Act of 1964, and the courts have noted that Title VII applies to education through Title IX of the Education Amendments of 1972. The act states that no person shall be denied an education in any activity receiving federal funds on the basis of sex. While most people think of Title IX as the law for equal access for women's athletic programs, the law increasingly is used for more sensitive areas of relationships.

In 1981 the Office of Civil Rights (OCR) issued a memorandum for institutions to formulate policies opposing sexual harassment, a grievance procedure, and procedures for prompt resolution. But it was not until the 1990s that awareness of such issues increased dramatically.

School board policies in Marion County, Florida, provide a sample of the kinds of considerations that are reasonable in thinking about sexual harassment:

1. Was the behavior in question based on sex?
2. Was the behavior (a) quid pro quo, such as a supervisor offering a benefit in return for sexual favors, or (b) hostile or abusive?
3. In the case of harassing behaviors, (a) is there a pattern of activity or (b) was a single act so outrageous as to constitute sexual harassment in and of itself.
4. Was the behavior unwelcome?
5. Was the behavior of a type that would offend, humiliate, or physically threaten a reasonable person?
6. Did the perpetrator know (or reasonably could be expected to know) that the behavior would be unwelcome?

Early sexual harassment suits tended to fall under the quid pro quo category. However, in 1992 the U.S. Supreme Court, using Title IX, determined that a girl or woman could bring suit — and be awarded damages — on the basis of a hostile environment being created in the school or workplace.[8] More recently, a circuit court suggested pithily, "A female student should not be required to run the gauntlet of sexual abuse in return for the privilege of being allowed to obtain an education."[9]

What about people who are "touchy-feely" by nature? The answer really lies in whether such attention, "normal" or not, is welcomed. Does this mean that teachers should never hug their students? Not necessarily. But it does mean that teachers need to be aware that some students may find such hugging uncomfortable. Normal, courteous, mutually respectful, pleasant, noncoercive interactions that are acceptable to both parties, regardless of whether the individuals are children or adults, are not considered to be harassment.

Sexual harassment cases can prove to be costly. In 1993 a Minnesota court awarded Jill Olson $40,000 for harassment. Olson had reported insults and sexual taunting to school authorities; they did nothing. The Minnesota Human Rights Commissioner said the award carried a simple message to all districts, "Take this stuff seriously."[10]

Many districts, taking note of the high awards being given in some cases, are choosing to settle out of court. An article in *Education Week* (15 January 1997) reported on a number of such settlements, including a California case in which the school district agreed to pay $250,000 to settle a lawsuit alleging that school officials failed to stop the sexual harassment of a junior high school girl by other students. In this case the student claimed to have reported several instances of harassment only to be told by school officials that "boys will be boys."

The same article also reported the case of a gay student who alleged that school officials failed to act on his complaints of abuse by other students. The school district settled out of court and, as in the previous case, admitted to no liability.

Negligent Hiring

Passing off an unsatisfactory employee by hiding the real reasons for his or her leaving can create a "dance of the lemons" that will haunt the school board that should have fired the unsatisfactory employee for cause in the first place. Consider a Pennsylvania case decided in 1994:

A music teacher, alleged to be sexually involved with a 12-year-old girl, a student in his class, was allowed to resign "for personal reasons." No record of the problem was placed in his file, and he was given a satisfactory evaluation. Fourteen years later, while teaching in another school district, the music teacher sexually abused a nine-year-old in the school band room.

The parents of the nine-year-old not only sued the school district that then employed the teacher, but also sued the teacher's previous district. Finding in favor of the plaintiffs, the court noted the first district's "affirmative cover-up" as showing "a policy, procedure, or custom of deliberate indifference" and said that the second district never would have hired the teacher had the circumstances of his resignation from the first district been known.[11]

In another case a California appeals court also ruled that school boards that fail to disclose full information about an employee's past performance can be held liable for future actions if that employee moves elsewhere. This case involved a middle school assistant principal. When the principal molested a 13-year-old student, the student's parents subsequently brought action against the principal, his current employer, and his former employers, who had neglected to mention that he had been disciplined for making sexual advances to students. The appeals court ruled that the duty not to defraud does extend to third parties (the former employers in this case). Furthermore, the previous employers were at fault under the Child Abuse Reporting Act for failing to report suspected child abuse.[12]

Clearly, the message to school boards is: Be honest. Negligent hiring can cause problems for a succession of employers over many years.

Notes

1. Meyer v. Nebraska, 262 U.S. 390 (1923).
2. Sullivan v. Meade Indep. School Dist. No. 101, 530 F.2d 799 (1976).
3. Brown v. Bathke, 566 F.2d 983 (1976).
4. Bowers v. Hardwick, 106 S.Ct. 2841 (1986).
5. Meritor Savings Bank v. Vinson, 477 U.S. 57 (1986).
6. Youngman v. Doerhoff, 890 S.W.2d 330 (Mo. Ct. App. 1994).
7. Davis v. Monroe County Bd. of Education, 119 S.Ct. 1661 (1999).
8. Franklin v. Gwinnet County Public Schools, 503 U.S. 60 (1992).
9. Dawn v. Monroe School Board, 74 F.3d 1186, 1194 (11th Cir. 1996).
10. Elaine Yaffe, "Expensive, Illegal, and Wrong: Sexual Harassment in Our Schools," *Phi Delta Kappan* 77 (November 1995): K4.
11. Doe v. Methacton Sch. Dist., 880 F. Supp. 380 (E.D. Pa. 1995).
12. Randi W. v. Livingston Union Sch. Dist., 48 Cal. Rptr. 2378 (Ct. App. 1995).

Chapter Thirteen

RELIGION AND THE SCHOOLS

No definition of religion exists in the Constitution, and the Supreme Court has expressly refused to define religion for First Amendment purposes. The First Amendment reads, "Congress shall make no law respecting an establishment of religion, or prohibiting the free exercise thereof." The first part of the amendment is called the Establishment Clause; the second is called the Free Exercise Clause. The Constitution's only other mention of religion is in Article VI with a statement that no religious test will be applied to those who seek to hold elected office.

The expression, "separation of church and state" is not used in the Constitution but was coined by Thomas Jefferson. It was not until 1879, more than a century later, in the case *Reynolds* v. *United States* that Thomas Jefferson's words "wall of separation of church and state" were used by the Supreme Court.

Tax Support for Religious Schools

In 1947 the Supreme Court ruled in *Everson* v. *Board of Education* that New Jersey's use of public funds for transporting parochial school children did not violate the First Amendment.[1] In 1968 the Court ruled in *Board of Education of Central School District No. 1* v. *Allen* that loaning textbooks to religious schools did not violate the Establishment Clause and that states could give aid as long as the aid supported secular services.[2] These decisions opened the floodgates for legislation, as some states took "secular services" to mean teachers' salaries, buildings, and other things. For example, Rhode Island gave salary supplements to teachers in religious schools who taught secular subjects; Pennsylvania went so far as to give direct aid to parochial schools.

In 1971 the Supreme Court heard *Lemon* v. *Kurtzman*, which challenged statutes enacted by Rhode Island and Pennsylvania to provide aid to parochial schools.[3] The Court found that statutes from both states were unconstitutional under the Establishment Clause because they created excessive entanglement between government and religion. The Court found it was clear that parochial schools have a religious mission. This ruling established the now famous *Lemon* test, which has three prongs to decide if a government policy toward religion is acceptable. To be constitutional, a statute or policy:

1. Must have a secular legislative purpose.
2. Must have a principal effect of neither advancing nor inhibiting religion.
3. Must not foster excessive entanglement of government with religion.

In the 1980s the wall began to crumble with a series of decisions. Taxpayers in Minnesota were allowed to deduct expenses for tuition, textbooks, and transportation for parochial school from their state income tax. The Individuals with Disabilities Education Act (IDEA) provided services for students attending religious high schools, as did Title I. In 2002 the Supreme Court ruled in *Zelman* v. *Simmons-Harris* that an Ohio program of vouchers for students who want to move from failing schools to parochial schools does not violate the Establishment Clause.[4] *Zelman* currently is the final word in a hot debate over vouchers, the Establishment Clause, and church-state relationships.

Religious Speech and School Prayer

Government may not bar or discriminate against religious expression. In 1985 Congress passed the Equal Access Act, which required schools that received federal aid to grant equal access to all non-curriculum-related student groups during non-instructional time. In the *Mergens* decision, the Court upheld the act and rejected the challenge that it violated the First Amendment. The Court stated that there is a crucial difference between government speech endorsing religion, which the Establishment Clause forbids, and private speech endorsing religion, which the Free Speech and Exercise Clauses protect.[5]

An important case in the 1990s, *Lamb's Chapel v. Center Moriches Union Free School District,* decided whether schools could exclude religious groups from using their property when nonreligious groups were allowed to do so. New York enacted a law that school boards may have regulations permitting school property to be used after hours for certain purposes, but not for religious meetings. An evangelical pastor and his church sought to use the school for a religious film about family values and child-rearing. The school denied access, and the church sued, claiming a violation of its First Amendment rights. The Court ruled that denying access to a speaker based on his or her views violates the First Amendment and that showing the film would not have violated the Establishment Clause because there was no realistic chance that the public could perceive that the district was endorsing religion.[6] If schools open their facilities to any group, then they must include all.

The rulings on access to school property do not apply to school-sponsored activities. For Bible reading, prayer, or meditation, the legality may depend on the time, place, and nature of the activity and whether there is official involvement in the activity. Several cases have determined that school-sponsored prayer is unconstitutional. In 1962 the Supreme Court determined in *Engle v. Vitale* that school-sponsored prayer is unconstitutional,[7] and in 1963 the Court ruled against classroom recitation of the Lord's Prayer and Bible verses.[8] These decisions were like an incendiary bomb for many religious groups, and a flurry of laws was enacted by legislatures to get around the rulings. Classroom periods of silence for student meditation, though affording opportunity for silent prayer, appear to be constitutional. However, if it is for the express purpose of promoting classroom prayer, it will be struck down. In *Wallace* v. *Jaffree*, the Court determined that the law was passed solely for the purpose of promoting classroom prayer, but suggested that moment-of-silence statutes would be constitutional if not religiously motivated and if school authorities remained neutral.[9] Later courts have upheld the neutral classroom meditation periods.

The lower courts have been seriously divided on the constitutionality of non-classroom prayer, such as during graduation ceremonies, extracurricular activities, or social events. Two Supreme Court decisions answered some of the questions. In *Lee* v. *Weisman*, the high school principal invited a rabbi to deliver a nondenominational prayer at a graduation ceremony. A student and her father unsuccessfully sued to block the prayer.[10] The student attended the ceremony but afterward appealed the ruling. The Supreme Court ruled 5 to 4 that the invocation violated the Establishment Clause.

The second decision, *Santa Fe* v. *Doe*, banned student prayer at football games.[11] In that case, a student was elected to recite a prayer over the public address system before home football games. The Court ruled that the school policy controlled the authorization of the prayer, and that the election by majority negated the role of any dissenter. The Court rejected the school district's categorization of the prayer as private speech.

Lower courts are divided on the constitutionality of the use of classical music with religious themes and Christmas music by school music groups. They also are divided on whether prayer should be allowed at school board meetings when students are attending. The Supreme Court has not ruled on these issues.

Holiday displays with religious origins have produced mixed rulings. Some lower courts have ruled that school holiday displays, plays, or songs with some religious elements are constitutional as long as the display serves a secular purpose and the religious elements do not dominate. The Supreme Court has not reconciled these cases.

However, in *Lynch* v. *Donnelly*, the Supreme Court ruled that the traditional acceptance of religious symbols and art on government property, including their own court room, were constitutional,[12] but this decision does not extend to religious displays or themes in public schools. For example, a plaque containing the Ten Commandments and religious art depicting the person and life of Jesus were considered to be displaying a religious message.

School Excusals for Religious Purposes

Excusing children from classes to pursue religious ends has received various treatment in courts. The Supreme Court struck down as an aid to religion the dismissal of students to go to another part of the school building for religious instruction, but it later ruled that students could be dismissed to attend religious studies away from the school.[13] The Supreme Court refused to review a ruling that found that a public school holiday that coincided with a major Christian holiday was constitutional, either as serving a secular purpose or as a religious accommodation.

The rights of teachers and students to be excused from normal school attendance for religious events depend on whether the school's need outweighs the individual's interest. For example, are substitutes available if a large number of teachers are out? However, Title VII of the Civil Rights Act mandates the reasonable accommodation of religion.

Religious Objections to Programs and Textbooks

Controversial programs and courses still draw fire. An inspection of court precedents shows that it is easier to have programs and courses banned if the arguments are based on the Establishment Clause, which shows the course gives favorable treatment to religions, than if they are based on the Free Exercise Clause, under which the objectors must prove that the programs coerce them to personally practice the religion.

Like courses, textbooks may be questioned for favoring or disfavoring religion. Complaints largely fail because they cannot meet the high burden of proving a constitutional violation. A Michigan court did not agree that *Slaughterhouse Five* presented an anti-religious message and ruled that teacher neutrality in discussing the book would overcome religious objections.[14] The Sixth Circuit ruled that students do not have to be excused from religiously objectionable material, and the Ninth Circuit avoided the issue by saying that students could opt out.

However, the Supreme Court has determined that it is unconstitutional for outside groups to distribute religious literature in public school classrooms. But it is constitutional for public schools to teach the Bible as literature and to use it as a source in history, literary, political, and comparative culture courses.

Of course, some of the most controversial cases arise from the teaching of evolution or creationism and intelligent design. Those cases are described in Chapter Five.

Guidelines for Educators

Religion will continue to be a hot topic. Making sure that one does not endorse one religion over another nor inhibit free expression of religions demands knowledge and planning. The following principles may help educators.

1. Policy decisions should include all stakeholders working to find common ground. Having no policies or those that the community does not support may turn into shouting matches and possible lawsuits. For example, in October 2005 the School Board of Hillsborough County Florida (Tampa) eliminated religious holidays from the school calendar, causing a public furor. Television programs reported that the removal was a reaction to a Muslim group's request for a holiday for the festival of Eid. However, the Muslim group said they fought to help keep the Jewish and Christian observances on the school calendar. The superintendent said the response was totally unexpected and the district was not prepared for it. A proactive, civil exploration of the issues could have prevented the firestorm.

2. Public schools may not inculcate nor inhibit religion. They must be places where religion and religious practices are treated with fairness and respect. Public schools must uphold the First Amendment and the rights of all religious faiths, including no faith. The curriculum should include studies about different religions as a part of a complete education.

3. Schools should respect the right of students to engage in religious activity and discussion. Individuals are free to pray, read the scriptures, discuss their faith, and invite others to join their religious groups. Only if the student's behavior is disruptive or infringes on the rights of others should the behavior be questioned.

4. Students are free to pray alone or in groups, as long as it is not disruptive and does not infringe on the rights of others. They may gather around the flagpole before school begins as long as the school does not sponsor the event and the students do not pressure other students to attend.

5. The Supreme Court did not rule against student prayer in school but against state-sponsored or state-organized prayer in public places. Government must be neutral among religions and between religions and non-religions. School officials may have a moment of silence as long as it does not promote prayer over other types of contemplation.

6. Lower courts are divided on whether a student may offer prayers at graduation exercises. Check the rules that apply in your state.

7. The public school may not sponsor a baccalaureate service, but parents and faith groups are free to sponsor the services. The school may announce this meeting as they would any other public service announcement.

8. Study about religion may be held wherever it arises in courses. A course on the Bible as history or on world religions may be offered in the curriculum, but it must be academic and not devotional.

9. Religious holidays offer opportunities to teach about religion in elementary and secondary schools. Teaching about religious holidays is different from celebrating the holidays. Religious symbols may be used as teaching aids, but only for the duration of the study. Sacred music may be sung or played as part of the school's academic program. Use of art, drama, music, or literature is permissible if it serves as part of an educational goal and is not used to promote religious beliefs.

10. When possible, accommodate the requests of parents for students to be excused from classroom discussions for religious reasons. If focused on a specific request or activity, the request should be granted to strike the balance between the student's religious freedom and school's curriculum.

11. Student religious clubs may have access to school facilities on the same basis as other non-curriculum-related clubs. Public schools are free to prohibit any club activities that are illegal or would cause disruption. Thus a student group wanting to form a Satanic club might be justifiably denied because such a club would cause a disruption.

12. Students may wear religious garb, such as head scarves or yarmulkes, to school. They may display religious messages on clothing to the same extent that other messages are permitted.

13. Students may distribute literature subject to reasonable time, place, and manner. The school may specify how and when this will occur.

14. Students may be released for off-campus religious instruction during the school day.[15]

Notes

1. Everson v. Board of Education, 330 U.S. 1 (1947).
2. Board of Education of Central School District No. 1 v. Allen, 392 U.S. 236 (1968).
3. Lemon v. Kurtzman, 403 U.S. 602 (1971).
4. Zelman v. Simmons-Harris, 536 U.S. 639 (2002).

5. Board of Educ. of Westside Community Schools v. Mergens, 496 U.S. 226 (1990).
6. Lamb's Chapel v. Center Moriches Union Free School District, 113 S. Ct. 2141 (1993).
7. Engle v. Vitale, 370 U.S. 421 (1962).
8. Abington v. Schempp, 372 U.S. 203 (1963).
9. Wallace v. Jaffree, 473 U.S. 38 (1985).
10. Lee v. Weisman, 505 U.S. 577 (1992).
11. Santa Fe Independent School District v. Doe, 530 U.S. 290 (2000).
12. Lynch v. Donnelly, 465 U.S. 668, 677 (1984).
13. Zorach v. Clauson, 343 U.S. 306 (1952).
14. Todd v. Rochester Comm. Schools, 200 N.W.2d 90 (Mich. 1972).
15. Some of these principles are adapted from "A Parent's Guide to Religion in the Schools," First Amendment Center, Nashville, Tenn., 2002.

Chapter Fourteen

FINANCE AND CONTRACTS

W hy should a teacher or principal want to know about school finance and collective bargaining? Principals are handed their budgets; teachers consider such matters out of their control. But it is unwise and perhaps even dangerous for teachers to invest their lives in a profession when they know nothing about its resources. And it is unwise for teachers to be aloof from the process of how money for schools is distributed. To misunderstand the process is to grapple with only petty issues but never to understand the big picture.

During the Watergate scandal, the reporters that broke the story were given great advice from the anonymous source called "Deep Throat." He told the reporters to "follow the money," explaining that, in politics, money reveals what is happening and who is benefiting. Likewise, the key to what is happening in schools is money.

In funding for education, federalism and decentralization is alive and well. The method of funding public schools can be described as chaotic and, in some places, unjust. This hodgepodge of finance began when schools were the concern of local communities. The Constitution did not mention education and left the responsibility to the states, many of which established local control of education. Money was raised by property taxes, and the struggle to do so met a lot of resistance. In a 1901 case, *Marion* v. *Alexander*, the Supreme Court of Kansas ruled that a district cannot levy taxes unless the legislature has laws enabling it to do so.[1] States passed laws that let the districts levy property taxes on real estate — homes and businesses — and sometimes personal property. Thus a district where there is lots of revenue will have more funds for its schools than will those in poorer districts.

Demetrio Rodriquez, a Mexican sheet metal worker in San Antonio, Texas, was appalled at conditions in his neighborhood school, Edgewood Elementary. Not only did the school lack books, certified teachers, and air conditioning, but the top two floors of the building were condemned. Only 10 minutes away at affluent Alamo Heights, children were taught by certified teachers in a nice building with lots of books. Edgewood residents paid one of the highest tax rates on property of any Texas community but were certainly not getting much for their investment. Rodriguez went to court claiming that this unfair system violated the U.S. constitutional provision of equal protection under the law.

It was 1968 when Rodriguez took the city of San Antonio to court. In 1973 the Supreme Court ruled against Rodriguez, citing the long history of local communities funding neighborhood schools.[2] The Court declared that education is not a fundamental right under the Constitution and that preserving local control is a legitimate reason to use the property tax system. They recognized that there were inequities, but it is up to the states to fix them.

In the mid-1980s Edgewood had neither typewriters nor a playground; Alamo Heights had computers and a swimming pool. Throughout Texas, per-pupil expenditures ranged from $2,112 to $19,333. In 1989, the school was again in the news. In *Edgewood* v. *Kirby*, the Supreme Court of Texas issued a unanimous decision that the legislature must come up with a fairer plan.[3]

State constitutions usually have strong equal protection clauses, and financial reformers have been successful in challenging reliance on property taxes under state provisions. For example, in California a group of citizens — dubbed the Robin Hood reformers because they wanted to take funds from wealthy districts and distribute them to poorer districts — were concerned about the glaring differences between Beverly Hills spending $1,232 per student and nearby Baldwin Park spending only $577 per student. They took their concern to the California Supreme Court, which ruled that education is a fundamental right under the California Constitution and that the property tax system violated equal protection of that right and thus was unconstitutional.[4] The victory was short-lived because many voters feared tax increases and passed Proposition 13 to limit the property tax.

Reformers in other states have sought to equalize funding through different programs. One is the foundation program, in which the state provides funds to insure that each student receives a minimal or foundation level of educational services. Another approach is the guaranteed tax base program that adds state funds to poorer districts, helping to reduce economic inequities.

Florida has a program called the Florida Education Finance Program (FEFP) that has a complicated formula for giving state funds to counties. In Florida, districts are coterminous with county lines; Florida has 67 counties and 67 school districts. The formula has a base student allocation that is multiplied by the weighted full-time equivalent students multiplied by the district cost-of-living differential. The districts must match the funds in property taxes but cannot go over a certain millage cap. Other specialties are built in the formula that would allow for army base closings or other financial emergencies.

Debates in some states have turned from financial input to education outcomes. A court in Kentucky declared the entire system of public schools was infirmed; and the state legislature enacted the Kentucky Education Reform Act (KERA) in 1990, which launched a new school curriculum, statewide performance tests, preschool programs for at-risk children, multiple grades in the same class, and economic incentives for educational progress. New York acted to provide students with desks and pencils, but not up-to-date science textbooks. Wyoming and Ohio went through years of litigation to define adequacy.

Collective Bargaining

Collective bargaining in the public sector has three general categories:

1. Mandatory subjects of bargaining that may include wages, hours, and other terms of employment. Sometimes what is mandatory is a matter of litigation. Generally agreed on is salary schedule, overtime, cost-of-living increases, fringe benefits, vacations, holidays, sick leave, retirement benefits, and so on.
2. Permissive subjects are such items as teacher workload, teacher hours, moving expenses, pay for unused sick leave, inservice education, and disciplinary actions against employees. Management retains the right to limit the scope of negotiable items.
3. Non-negotiable items are things that are designated by the state. For example, the number of days required in school.

The bargaining unit represents all teachers within the district, even those who are not members of the union. The union also provides insurance coverage and legal counsel for teachers who have difficulties. Usually a grievance procedure for questionable practices within the school is available, and usually it is effective in solving problems.

Some states have very strong unions and fight effectively for their teachers. For example, Michigan teachers have very strong unions. Other states and districts have weak unions, and bargaining is more difficult. Florida is a right-to-work state; teachers cannot strike. But the union is a friend to its members if one gets in trouble with parents or administrators. The state in which one lives has a great effect on the strength and benefit of the union.

School finance is a hodgepodge of ways of doing things because state laws organizing schools are so different. Until the Supreme Court rules on an all-encompassing principle, it probably will remain as it is now.

Notes

1. Marion Railway Co. v. Alexander Supreme Court of Kansas, 163 Kan. 72 (1901).
2. San Antonio Independent School District v. Rodriguez, 411 U.S. 1 (1973).
3. Edgewood Independent School District v. Kirby, 777 S.W.2d 391 (Tex. 1989).
4. Serrano v. Priest, 487 P.2d 1241 (1971).

Chapter Fifteen

SOURCES FOR FURTHER RESEARCH

Perhaps one of the best ways to guard against lawsuits is to stay informed about the law. As legal issues come to light, laws change and interpretations of laws change. A good example is one I touched on in Chapter Twelve. Although strong laws regarding sexual harassment had been on the books since the 1970s, they did not receive much attention until the 1990s. How can educators keep abreast of change? Following are several sources of information.

Periodicals. Each issue of the *Phi Delta Kappan* contains a regular feature, titled "Courtside," written by Perry Zirkel, who presents current issues in education law. The clearly described cases are chosen from a broad field of interest to educators.

The journals of the National Association of Secondary School Principals (NASSP) and the National Association of Elementary School Principals (NAESP) both feature legal perspectives in each issue. The same is true for *Educational Leadership*, the journal of the Association for Supervision and Curriculum Development. The *American School Board Journal* is written from a school board point of view, but many articles are pertinent to educators' interests generally.

Most of the national subject-area organizations (for example, National Council of Teachers of English) produce journals that contain, at least from time to time, articles related to legal issues. The same is true for athletic and coaches organizations. And there are a wealth of specialized periodicals, such as *West's Education Law*, the *Journal of Law and Education*, and *Legal Notes for Education*, many of which are available in university libraries.

Education Week and *Teacher Magazine* are weekly and monthly periodicals, respectively, that report on the courts and legislatures. *Education Week*'s focus is K-12; its counterpart for colleges and universities is the *Chronicle of Higher Education*.

A number of these organizations and periodicals also maintain sites on the World Wide Web. Phi Delta Kappa International's URL is www.pdkintl.org, for example. Education Week Online can be found at www.edweek.org.

Organizations. In addition to the various professional associations, some other organizations can be helpful in keeping up on changes in various laws. An example is the Education Law Association (ELA), formerly the National Organization on Legal Problems in Education (NOLPE). Their headquarters is in Dayton, Ohio. The association was founded in 1954 to provide an unbiased forum and to publish newsletters, books, and monographs. They also sponsor an annual national conference.

In addition to the websites mentioned previously, others sponsored by a variety of organizations may be useful. For example, Seamless is a consumer law site, but it can be searched for education law rulings: www.seamless.com. EDLAW publishes books and produces seminars specifically related to the Individuals with Disabilities Education Act (IDEA) and Section 504.

Books. A number of books about aspects of education law are published each year, some written to address perennial issues. The more comprehensive the book, the less current it is likely to be, given the time required to publish a book-length work. Nonetheless, several books are worth noting. Alexander and Alexander's *American Public School Law* (West, 1997) is an example. They also wrote *The Law of Schools, Students, and Teachers in a Nutshell* (West, 1995).

Perry Zirkel's *The Law of Teacher Evaluation* (Phi Delta Kappa Educational Foundation, 1996) was published in cooperation with NOLPE. Zirkel, with co-authors Sharon Nalbone Richardson and Steven S. Goldberg, also wrote *A Digest of Supreme Court Decisions Affecting Education*, 4th edition (Phi Delta Kappa Educational Foundation, 2001).

More current cases can be found in the *Desktop Encyclopedia of American School Law from Data Research*, which is updated annually. The Education Law Association also publishes an annual *Yearbook of Education Law*.

Conferences. A number of universities and associations hold conferences dealing with legal issues in education. For example, the Franklin Pierce Law Center in Concord, New Hampshire, holds an annual law seminar for people interested in school law. Information can be found online at www.fplc.edu. Many conferences are announced in either *Education Week* or the *Chronicle of Higher Education*.

Websites. Several legal search engines and directories are open to the general public. They are easy to navigate and can help users find laws pertaining to basic topics. Some of the more useful sites include:

- All Law: www.alllaw.com
- American Law Sources On-line (ALSO): www.lawsource.com/also/
- Cornell University: supct.law.cornell.edu/supct
- Council on Law in Higher Education: www.clhe.org
- Findlaw: www.findlaw.com
- Hieros Gamos: hg.org/hg.html
- Law.com: www.law.com
- MegaLaw.com: www.megalaw.com
- Virtual Law Library: www.law.indiana.edu
- Lexis Nexis: www.lexis-nexis.com (by subscription, but many libraries subscribe)

Following are sources for the U.S. Supreme Court, federal courts, and federal government sources:

- Federal courts: www.uscourts.gov
- FedLaw: legal.gsa.gov
- Federal Register: access.gpo.gov/su_doc/aces/aces140.html
- U.S. Senate: www.senate.gov
- The White House: www.whitehouse.gov

Locating and Reading Laws and Cases

Educators who are located near a major university should have no trouble doing basic legal research, and many county court houses also have a law library that is available to the public.

Law librarians are indispensable for the uninitiated, but readers of cases can soon get the hang of legal citation, which is fairly universal within the United States. For example, in the citation 419 U.S. 565, the 419 is the volume; U.S. stands for the book, *United States Reports*; and 565 is the page number. Another example: In *Arnold* v. *Hayslett*, 655 S.W.2d 941 (Tenn. 1983), the case of "Arnold versus Hayslett" can be found in volume 655 of *Southwestern Reporter*. The notation 2d means the second series of this report. The opinion begins on page 941, and the case was decided in Tennessee in 1983.

The more cases one reads, the better one gets at understanding the legal language. Following are several questions to consider when reading a case that are suggested by John Strope in his book, *School Activities and the Law* (NASSP, 1984):

- Who were the parties? the plaintiff? the defendant? (If the case goes to appeal, who was the appellate? the appellee?)
- What were the legal issues?
- What were the facts, or circumstances, of the case?
- What relief was requested? Did the plaintiffs want money damages? an injunction?
- Was this a lower court or an appellate court decision?
- What were the plaintiff's legal arguments?

- What were the defendant's legal arguments?
- Who won? What was the court's reasoning to support the result?
- What message should the reader get from the case?

Educators would do well to learn as much as they can about school law. One way to do so, in addition to individual effort, is to take a school law class. Many states and school districts require educators to take continuing education classes in order to renew state licenses, and so a school law class can be put to good use in a couple of ways. Many administrators are required to take a school law class in order to meet initial licensing requirements; but if that class was 10 or more years ago, then it is a good idea to take the class again. Laws do change, and there is little point in hanging onto outdated information.

It is hoped that educators who read this book will be intrigued by the law and will want to know more. I have attempted to provide a starting point — actually, a number of starting points — for further learning.

About the Author

Evelyn B. Kelly is an educator, writer, and community activist living in Marion County, Florida. She has been a science and health educator and an adjunct professor of education at Saint Leo University.

Kelly is past president of the Florida Chapter of the American Medical Writers Association and is a member of the National Association of Science Writers and the American Society of Journalists and Authors. She holds a B.A. in microbiology and English from the University of Tennessee, a master's degree in religion, and a Ph.D. in curriculum and instruction from the University of Florida.

She has written six books and more than 400 articles on health and education for various magazines and journals. Her most recent book is *Obesity*, published by Greenwood Press. She also is the author of several Phi Delta Kappa fastbacks, as well as the previous edition of *Legal Basics*.

Kelly and her husband live on a farm in Ocala, Florida. They have four children.